Gilbert Stuart, painter of George Washington and other founding fathers, at one time regarded in England as the probable successor of Sir Joshua Reynolds, once shuddered away from a self-portrait he had started to please his bride. Here is the portrait the artist himself could not face, made as he would have made it, frank, without flattery, profound, and soul-stirring.

Born in poverty in Rhode Island, Stuart became through his art the intimate of the great of two continents. Yet he never abandoned his disdain for worldly rank, his fascination with character. He made huge sums in England, but spent even more on dissipation. Prison yawned for him, and he fled his creditors. During thirty-five American years, he painted with brilliance, creating a unique portrait manner. His rank as an artist was never questioned, but his nerves would not quiet. He drank, fought with his wife, and tortured his children. He died as he had lived; famous and bankrupt.

⁊⁊   ⁊⁊   ⁊⁊

James Thomas Flexner has written brilliantly about American painting in such books as **First Flowers of Our Wilderness** and **The Light of Distant Skies.** Born in New York City in 1908, he has been a **Herald Tribune** reporter, a Lowell Lecturer, a Guggenheim Fellow, a **teacher** at Columbia, and the author of biographies, including **The Traitor and the Spy.**

GREAT LIVES IN BRIEF
A New Series of Biographies

ACCURACY
BREVITY CLARITY
MULTUM
IN PARVO

HENRY FORD *by Roger Burlingame*

MAHATMA GANDHI *by Vincent Sheean*

ALEXANDRE DUMAS *by André Maurois*

HANS CHRISTIAN ANDERSEN *by Rumer Godden*

CHARLES DARWIN *by Ruth Moore*

JULIUS CÆSAR *by Alfred Duggan*

JAMES J. HILL *by Stewart Holbrook*

ELIZABETH I *by Donald Barr Chidsey*

NAPOLEON III *by Albert Guérard*

GILBERT STUART *by James Thomas Flexner*

These are BORZOI BOOKS
Published by ALFRED A. KNOPF *in New York*

GILBERT STUART

Gilbert Stuart

A GREAT LIFE IN BRIEF

BY

James Thomas Flexner

New York   ALFRED A. KNOPF   1955

L. C. catalog card number: 55–6218

© JAMES THOMAS FLEXNER, *1955*

THIS IS A BORZOI BOOK,
PUBLISHED BY ALFRED A. KNOPF, INC.

FIRST EDITION

TO WILLIAM SAWITZKY

1879–1947

Pioneer student of early American art

CONTENTS

CONTENTS

GILBERT STUART

CHAPTER ONE

A WILD BOY

LIKE a true believer entering a shrine, John Neal tiptoed reverently into Gilbert Stuart's Boston studio.
The more art is banished from the main current of
national life by utilitarian pursuits, the more holy it
seems to its votaries. In the roaring 1820's when the
energies of the nation were absorbed in the growing
settlements beyond the mountains, Neal, who aspired to be a painter, thought of Gilbert Stuart as a
god. Was not Stuart recognized as the greatest artist
in America? Had he not preserved the features of
Washington for all future ages? Humbly Neal ad-
vanced toward the end of his pilgrimage.

He passed the threshold with eyes modestly down-
cast, but when he looked up, the worship in his expression gave way to surprise. He saw before him a
furious-looking old man whose disheveled clothes
were encrusted with snuff and one of whose feet was
bound up because of gout. A huge mouth curved
powerfully downward among the sagging muscles of
his lower face; bloodshot eyes stared with unpleasant
intensity from behind red lids. This terrifying countenance was dominated by a tremendous nose whose
purple-red veins proclaimed its owner a perpetual
drinker. When Neal asked incredulously if this was

Gilbert Stuart, the corners of the mouth lifted into a
sarcastic smile. However, the voice in which the
painter admitted his identity was suave and had the
well-bred London sound that Americans associated
with culture. Neal was reassured by the courtliness
with which he was shown to a chair; it was a mistake,
he decided, to judge by first appearance.

After a few minutes, the painter excused himself
and limped to a closet. Neal expected him to bring
out some delicately tinted portrait for them to exclaim
over together, but Stuart emerged with a half-gallon
jug in which red liquid swished sibilantly. Swinging
the jug over his shoulder, he poured two brimming
glasses, "like cider-switchel at haying time," Neal remembered. When the lad hesitated about drinking his
portion, the painter told him not to worry: the Madeira was good; it had been twice around the Cape.

Neal reported years later that he could not believe
his eyes and ears. It was impossible that a denizen of
the high kingdom of art should descend to such vul-
garity. Suddenly he remembered Stuart's reputation
for practical jokes. Of course, genius had to have its
vagaries; Neal smiled wanly, but his smile faded when
Stuart tossed off half a tumbler at one swallow and
peremptorily ordered him to drink up. The frightened
youngster explained that he had been brought up on
"the plainest of wholesome food"; liquor had never
touched his lips. At this Stuart laughed raucously and

winked, as much as to say "Can't you trust me?" He tossed off a whole tumblerful this time, and wished for better acquaintance.

Then Stuart made a series of the vilest puns, and laughed at them immoderately. He criticized the saintly burghers of Boston, calling the statutes by which they regulated their neighbors "blue laws" which showed "the bigotry and fanaticism of the day." Not a word of art came from between the heavy lips; the old man, who obviously enjoyed shocking his visitor, talked about wine. He boasted that he was the best judge of wines "on this side of the water," and told innumerable stories to demonstrate it. Neal recalled how Stuart gloated over the gay parties he had attended in Philadelphia, where he had belonged to a club of a dozen or twenty good fellows "who were a law unto themselves." Once a year they got together, each bringing a bottle for every guest, a dozen or twenty, according to the number who were coming, and it was a point of honor to drink up every drop before dawn.

All the while he talked, Stuart was filling his capacious nostrils from a snuffbox "nearly as large round as the top of a small hat." This snuffbox, one of the biggest ever seen in America, was famous in Stuart's circle; after he had mislaid it, a friend hired a porter with a wheelbarrow to bring it back. On another occasion, when Stuart was entertaining two young painters less prudish than Neal, one of them asked him for a pinch. "I will give it to you," Stuart replied, "but I advise you not to take it. Snuff-taking is a pernicious, vile, dirty habit, and, like all bad habits, to be carefully avoided." [1]

"Your practice," the young painter remembers he replied, "contradicts your precept, Mr. Stuart."

"Sir, I can't help it. Shall I tell you a story? You were neither of you ever in England, so I must describe an English stagecoach of my time. It was a large vehicle of the coach kind, with a railing around the top to secure outside passengers, and a basket behind for baggage and such travelers as could not be elsewhere accommodated. In such a carriage, full within, loaded on the top, and an additional *unfortunate* stowed with the stuff in the basket, I happened to be traveling in a dark night, when coachee contrived to overturn us all—or, as they say in New York, dump us—in a ditch. We scrambled up, felt our legs and arms to be convinced that they were not broken, and finding on examination that inside and outside passengers were tolerably whole (on the whole), someone thought of the poor devil who was shut with the baggage in the basket. He was found apparently senseless, and his neck twisted awry. One of the passengers, who had heard that any dislocation

---

[1] The spelling and punctuation in all quotations have been modernized.

might be remedied if promptly attended to, seized on the corpse with a determination to untwist the man's neck and set his head straight on his shoulders. Accordingly, with an iron grasp he clutched him by the head, and began pulling and twisting by main force. He appeared to have succeeded miraculously in restoring life, for the dead man no sooner experienced the first wrench than he roared vociferously: 'Let me alone! Let me alone! I'm not hurt; I was born so!' Gentlemen," added Stuart, "I was born so." He took an enormous pinch of snuff. "I was born in a snuff mill."

The painter's father, also named Gilbert Stuart, was a Scotch snuff-grinder who in his early thirties had emigrated from Perth to Rhode Island. Although his descendants made up, to enhance their social position, romantic tales about his forebears, he came from too humble a stock to have any recorded genealogy. His family never figured in the life of his son, even when the painter was as a youth marooned in Scotland and much in need of help.

The elder Stuart must have reached America in 1750 or earlier, since on May 21, 1751 he was married to a Newport girl, Elizabeth Anthony. Her great-grandfather, John Anthony, of Hampstead, England, had in 1634 come to Rhode Island, where he continued his old profession of innkeeper, became prosperous, and inaugurated a line of farmers

which slowly descended in worldly importance. Elizabeth's father was not well-off, not poor, not important, not insignificant—one of those individuals who
form the backbone of long-settled rural communities.
He married Susan Hefferman, sired seven children,
and died at the age of fifty-two, when Elizabeth was
eighteen, leaving behind no considerable estate. The
girl, who grew into "a very handsome woman," was
twenty-three when she married her thirty-five-year-old
snuff-grinder.

According to Newport gossip, her husband's presence in America was indirectly due to the failure of
Bonnie Prince Charlie's rebellion in Scotland. Dr.
Thomas Moffatt, a learned Boerhavian physician, was
forced to flee to Rhode Island. When he found that
his aristocratic manners so annoyed the Quakers there
that they would not have him in their houses, he decided that his graces were more important to him than
his profession; he gave up medicine, and cast around
for another means of livelihood. Noticing that the
snuff he bought was imported from Scotland, he determined to set up a snuff mill, and finding no one in
America capable of building one, imported the elder
Gilbert Stuart.

There was a considerable delay after the artisan's
arrival, in establishing the mill. It was November 5,
1751 when Stuart, who described himself as "millwright," entered into a partnership with Moffatt,

"physician," and Edward Cole, "gentleman," to erect on a tidal river near Narragansett an "engine for the manufacture of snuff," the first, it is said, in New England.

After the structure was completed, the Stuarts lived in the upper stories. In April 1752 a son, James, was born; he soon died. The following year, Ann came, and then, on December 3, 1755, Gilbert Jr. The future painter remained the only boy and the youngest child.

Decades later, Stuart amused himself by telling people he met in England that he first saw the light "six miles from Pottawoone and ten miles from Pappasquash and about four miles from Conanicut and not far from the spot where the famous battle with the warlike Pequots was fought." When asked what province of India he came from, he was enchanted.

Since the mill was built on a sharp slope, the infant painter saw from his upper-story bedroom the pond rippling and glowing, almost level with his eyes. Then, just by the window, turbulence took over. The water cascaded with a shout down the side of the dam, striking the blades of the wheel, which, as it revolved, set up a great groaning of machinery that rocked the floor on which he stood. In this world of sound and movement the little boy soon established himself as his own master. His elder sister doted on him, as did his easygoing and impractical parents.

Stuart's father was so absent-minded that once, when he and his wife were riding to church on the same horse, he dropped the lady off without noticing. And she was so good-humored that she was not angry as she sat on the road where she had landed, but rather smiled to think how surprised her husband would be when he found her gone. She watched the millwright jog gaily round a bend, there was the silence of heat and birds singing, and then suddenly the clatter of hoofs. Stuart appeared at a gallop, leaning eagerly over his horse's neck. "God's-my-life!" he cried. "Are you hurt?"

The usual stories are told of Gilbert's precocity. When he was five, his daughter relates, he drew on the earth with a stick a perfect likeness of a neighbor. Family tradition also records a holiday excursion to a hanging as an example of his early powers of observation. The shy hangman, who had hidden his identity with a sheet draped from head to ankle, mystified everyone but the babe on Mr. Stuart's shoulder; Gilbert reported who it was. "I know him," the innocent lisped, "by his sues."

Mrs. Stuart decided that so brilliant an infant must be taught Latin before he was well out of swaddling-clothes. Since no one in the neighborhood knew any Latin, she sent to Newport for a primer and, though she had never seen a word of the strange language,

essayed to teach little Gilbert herself. Of course he
did not learn very much.

Gilbert's father, we are told, "was remarkable for
his ingenuity and his quiet, inoffensive life"; he lacked
the gift for making money. When Colonial industry
proved unable to supply any bottles into which his
snuff could be packed, he was in despair, until Moffatt
suggested the substitution of beeves' bladders. Then
gaiety returned to the clanking mill, but not for long;
the bladders were not immediately popular. Heart-
broken, Stuart sold his share in the mill when Gilbert
was six, and settled in Newport on a scrap of property
his wife had inherited. Moffat then proceeded to make
money from the mill. Thus it always was with the
well-meaning mechanic. According to his grand-
daughter, he later invented a machine for loading
ships which made someone else rich and did him no
good whatsoever.

Gilbert was to describe his family's Newport house
as "a hovel on Bannister's wharf." Like his artistic
predecessor John Singleton Copley, Stuart spent his
boyhood in a tobacco shop on the seafront of a mari-
time city; but while Copley had trembled behind
windowpanes, Stuart was forever out on the streets
leading a gang of urchins in outrageous pranks.

He attended an Episcopalian charity school which
had been founded in 1742 as part of Trinity Church

by Bishop Berkeley "to teach ten poor boys their grammar and mathematics gratis." The master had to be ordained, and thus the Reverend George Bisset was in charge, but the actual instruction was given by John Ernest Knotchell, "a German gentleman, learned and severe," who lived in the schoolyard. Knotchell's grammar, his mathematics, his learning and severity repelled Stuart, but he had a skill which the boy found fascinating: he was the church organist. The teacher found he could keep his wildest pupil quiet by seating him at the fine instrument which Bishop Berkeley had donated to the congregation. When Stuart revisited Newport as an old man, the only landmark of his childhood that brought him contentment was the organ-loft.

School served Stuart principally as a reservoir of companions he could lead astray. Books were forgotten while he frolicked with Arthur Browne, later a famous English attorney, and Benjamin Waterhouse, who was to introduce vaccination into the United States. The three bright youngsters prowled on the docks, practicing oaths and trying to spit like veterans. Or, curled up on bulkheads over the bright water, they would sail in their imaginations to that almost impossible homeland which their parents described to them. They were all, Waterhouse tells us, "inspired with the same ardent desire to visit Europe."

Stuart used to amuse his friends during his later

years by saying that he and another boy named Channing had sworn revenge on a shoemaker who had got them into trouble. They sneaked up to his open window on a dark night, and one boy fired a gun while the other squirted blood they had stolen from a butcher onto the cobbler's bald head. The shoemaker rolled over among his lasts and lapstones, crying that he was murdered. Hiding in the long grass, swallowing down their mirth, the urchins watched his wife run in and scream for help; they saw the doctor, who had arrived with his coattails flying, approach the corpse gravely, wash off the blood, and then stare in amazement. They were so entranced that they did not set off for their homes in time to make a clean getaway; the miraculously revived cadaver rushed out to complain, and as the boys were found in bed with their shoes on, they were adjudged guilty and roundly beaten with a birch. Stuart loved to say that he had called on their victim years later and reminded him of the incident. The shoemaker shook his head. "If you're as good a man as you were a bad boy, you're a devilish clever fellow."

Waterhouse remembered that Gilbert was "a very capable, self-willed boy who, perhaps on that account, was indulged in everything, being an only son, handsome and forward and habituated at home to have his own way in everything, with little or no control from the easy, good-natured father." Rebellion was in

the Stuart heritage. Although there appears to be no
foundation for the story that Gilbert's father fought at
Culloden, his sympathies were undoubtedly with
Prince Charlie, and most of his American friends were
Scottish exiles. He seems to have become a more violent rebel after he had been in Rhode Island for several
years; he changed the spelling of his family name from
"Stewart" to "Stuart," and added to his son's name,
some time after his baptism, the middle name of
"Charles," which the lad bore proudly for a while before he discarded it entirely. Certainly the talk around
the dinner table did not teach slavish obedience to
constituted authority.

CHAPTER TWO

A PRIMITIVE PAINTER

THE FUTURE artist was stricken with an illness which so affected his eyesight that it was feared he would go blind. When Dr. William Hunter, the leading physician of the Scotch community, was called in, the special tragedy of the situation was clear to him, for the boy who was now lying in a darkened room had covered the walls of his family's little house with drawings. Lacking paints and a brush, he had used a rotting stone or a lump of clay, and yet there was vitality in the designs that made Hunter study them with admiration. The doctor, who owned paintings which he fondly hoped were "originals and uniques" by Salvator Rosa, considered himself a connoisseur; he resolved to help the boy become an artist—that is, if his eyesight could be restored. Stuart recovered and, as soon as he did, Hunter gave him brushes and colors, commissioned him to paint two spaniels lying under a table.

Hunter's presumed Rosas were far from being the only sources of art in Newport. Religious toleration had joined with a capacious harbor to make the city a great trading-center; more than three thousand seamen were employed in locally owned ships that crowded wharves stretching for a mile along the waterfront. The merchants were wealthy—one boasted that, to

avoid ostentation, he had cut his staff to seventy servants—and they imported from Europe in their own
boats luxuries suited to their class: paintings as well as
furniture and fine wines. Isaac Hart, a pillar of the
Jewish community, was convinced that his bust portrait of Tsar Peter I was by the famous London society
painter Sir Godfrey Kneller. Another merchant, John
Bannister, owned, among many portraits of famous
Europeans, a presumptive self-portrait by Van Dyck;
also a picture, locally considered beautiful, of "Cleo-
patra dying in an oval frame." The Scotch exiles particularly admired the collection of the elder Stuart's
former partner, Dr. Moffatt, which featured a heroic
painting of Bonnie Prince Charlie and, for contrast, a
depiction of the King's brother, the Duke of Cumberland, as "a butcher with a cleaver in his hand."

Newport society was extremely aristocratic in tone,
and the Stuarts were not among those who, in the
words of the rector of Trinity Church, "moved in
higher spheres"; yet the Colonials everywhere were
eager to encourage artists, and as soon as Dr. Hunter
made the boy's ambitions known, the prodigy was undoubtedly admitted, even if only by a servant, to the
mansions where the imported pictures hung. However, he seems to have been less moved by the European images that had little reference to his own crude
sketches and to the world he knew than by the example of a man in his own sphere, the instrument-

maker's son Samuel King, who practiced house- and portrait-painting as a sideline to his father's trade. Likenesses created by King some years later reveal that he was completely uninspired, yet he worked in the crabbed, linear style Stuart was to practice when he himself became a professional portraitist.

The training Stuart gave himself was at first completely conventional for an American beginner: he copied engravings and drew faces in black lead. Then, when he was thirteen or fourteen, a meteor, albeit a very small one, flashed into the artistic skies of Newport.

Cosmo Alexander was an elegant Scot who had fought for the Pretender, but he was not an exile: it was rumored that he was a spy sent by the British to keep an eye on the obstreperous Colonials. For his part, he declared he was traveling for his health and to recover some lost lands belonging to his family. He admitted in the parlors of the Scotch colony that he was an expert painter, that he had studied in Italy and was a member of the Society of Artists in London, but added that he was too much of a gentleman to make painting a profession: he merely sketched for his amusement. He waited until he had been adequately persuaded before he set up a studio, well supplied, as Waterhouse remembered, with "cameras and optical glasses for taking perspective views." These were devices for throwing miniature images into a darkened box where they could be traced by hand with little trouble: modern cameras in everything except the presence of light-sensitive film.

"Dr. Hunter," the physician's son was to boast, "placed Stuart under the tuition of his friend Alexander." This meant, according to Waterhouse, that the boy was given instruction "in the grammar of art," in "drawing and the groundwork of the palette." Soon Alexander was so impressed that he took Stuart into his studio.

Late in 1770 or early in 1771 the lad accompanied his master on a painting tour through the South, and then destiny presented him with the ultimate favor, a trip to the almost fabulous world across the ocean whence art came. Alexander took him to Scotland. For a while Stuart prospered, following in the wake of his elegant master, who may even have sent him to school for short periods of time. But on August 25, 1772 Alexander died at Edinburgh. As he felt himself failing, he begged a friend to take care of Stuart.

According to Waterhouse, this friend was Sir George Chambers, an individual otherwise unidentified. Stuart's modern biographer, William T. Whitley, points out that Alexander had a brother-in-law named Sir George Chalmers. Chalmers had been a pupil of Allan Ramsay, but was an extremely feeble painter; he claimed to be a baronet, but his estate had been forfeited by a Jacobin ancestor. Waterhouse states that Chambers died almost at once. Whitley points out that, although Chalmers lived until 1791, he was too poor to be of much assistance to anyone.

Whether Chambers or Chalmers, Stuart's new guardian did not help him for long. The sixteen-year-old boy was abandoned in Edinburgh with no means of livelihood except his very inexpert brush. He signed himself "Charles Stuart," appealing to Scottish patriotism, and does seem to have obtained a commission or two, but probably was paid very little. The gay youngster who had been the darling of his family, the prodigy whom the Scottish colony of Newport had admired and caressed, now walked the streets of a strange and hostile city, his pockets and his belly empty, his feet sore. Rarely during the hours and hours of autobiographical conversation with which he filled his later years did he refer to those months of abject misery, and his daughter tried to gloss them over by saying that he spent two years at the University of Glasgow, long enough to acquire "a classical taste." But the records of that institution are innocent of his name.

Hungry, footsore days massed into months, and still there seemed no way out for the lonely boy: no money to go home with, nothing to eat if he stayed. Finally he seized a desperate expedient; he enlisted before the mast on a collier bound for Nova Scotia. The sea was a brutal mistress in those days. Men were

beaten and starved and worked to the limit of endur-
ance. We can see the young painter clinging to a
yardarm over the black sea, weeks of terrible sailing
behind him, weeks more ahead, his thoughts tumbling
sickishly to the unremitting beat of waves and to the
curses of the boatswain coming up from below.

When Stuart reached Newport at last, he could
not make himself describe his trip home even to his
best friend. "What his treatment was I never could
learn," writes Waterhouse. "I only know that it required a few weeks to equip him with suitable cloth-
ing to appear on the streets, or to allow any one of his
former friends, save the writer, to know of his return
home. Suffice it to say that it was such as neither Gilbert Stuart, father or son, ever thought proper to mention."

Stuart's family, for so long completely obscure,
was now in a position to help his worldly rise. His
mother's much younger brother, Joseph Anthony, had
gone to sea and risen to the rank of captain. Then he
became a favorite of Aaron Lopez, the Portuguese Jew
who had amassed a fortune in Newport as the pioneer
manufacturer and distributor of spermaceti candles, a
luxury made from whale oil. Anthony had bought
boats of his own, and, although he kept his close connection with Lopez, had moved his base of operations
to Philadelphia, where he allied himself with the great
mercantile firm of Stocker and Wharton.

When visiting Newport, Anthony was amazed to see hanging on the Stuarts' wall a likeness of his mother, who had never been painted in her lifetime. Told that young Gilbert, just back from Scotland, had painted it from memory, he commissioned pictures of himself, his wife, and his two children; he showed them to his business connections. Lopez ordered his own likeness and a double portrait of his wife and child; Lopez's brother-in-law and partner Jacob Rodriquez Ribera followed suit, and soon it became fashionable to patronize Stuart. Next to his presumed Van Dyck, John Bannister hung portraits of a more personal nature by the local prodigy.

"Our aspiring artist," writes Waterhouse, "had as much business as he could turn his hands to, and the buoyancy of his spirits kept pace with his good fortune." The horrible days in Scotland seemed forgotten while the gay young man dashed off portraits, flirted with the ladies, taught himself to play various musical instruments, and tried his hand at composing. "Once," his friend continues, "he attempted to enrapture me by a newly studied classical composition. I exerted all the kind attention I could muster up for the occasion, until his sharp eye detected by my physiognomy that I did not much relish it. He colored, sprang up in a rage, and striding back and forth the floor, vociferated: 'You have no more taste for music than a jackass! And it is all owing to your stupid Quaker education!' "

Deciding that he had the gift of prophecy, Stuart secretly recorded his forecasts in what he called a "Book of Judges," and waited for them to come true. When they failed to do so, he admitted to Waterhouse that high in the list of his predictions was Waterhouse's own death at an early age.

The brash young man did not hesitate to use the painting style he had learned from Alexander, the art he had seen in Scotland, as no more than a springboard for his own provincial visions. Alexander had been a graceful workman, if a weak one. He had sought natural poses: a lady fingering a piano; a gentleman opening a pouch. His was a sugary sort of realism; people were shown as they might have been in life, except that they were more elegant and prettier. Although his figures had no existence in space and were visualized with no vitality of imagination, the technique was smooth enough to hide their emptiness from a casual viewer. And the colors were not lacking in charm.

Stuart sensed that such work was trivial; it glossed over the truth that his own eyes saw. Yet he was not sure where the artificiality lay, where to dig for verity. He followed his instincts, and it is amazing how often the experiments he tried in his early pictures presaged the conclusions of his prime.

Typical of his Newport work was his portrait of

Mrs. Lopez with her small son Joshua beside her. As
he was to do all through his career, Stuart planned his
colors to emphasize the flesh tones, which in this case
had an olive glow. He caught the tint exactly and
keyed it into a color scheme based on the contrast between coal-black hair and a symphony of blues: a
dark-blue dress with lighter-blue highlights; a blue-
gray background shading behind the heads to a more
creamy azure, and suddenly enlivened with bright-
blue touches in a lace cap.

Very conspicuous was the contrast between the
painting of the heads and that of the bodies. Even
then, at the opening of his career, Stuart revealed his
lifelong fascination with faces and indifference to figures and costumes. He showed Mrs. Lopez's torso as
shrunken and completely flat, but tried desperately to
understand the shape of the head, to express weight
and three-dimensional form. His European training
was indicated by the way he kept the features in a
bright light and gathered the shadows together into a
few masses, but he applied this knowing technique
with such innocent violence that the shadows over-
modeled, giving the heads the strangely astringent
quality, as if the skin were shrinking on the flesh, that
was typical of Stuart's Newport pictures.

Despite his emphasis on faces, he was not successful in achieving likenesses. As Alexander had done, he
tended to make heads square and pudgy; he drew

eyebrows and eyes and mouths in a manner somewhat similar to his master's; yet he had broken so completely with the Scot's approach that such borrowed forms had lost their illusionistic naturalism. Like a broad-jumper who returns to the starting-line before beginning his second leap, Stuart has receded to the approach of self-taught primitives. Mrs. Lopez's face has been metamorphosed into a design grounded in the repetition of shapes. Her oval mass of hair complements the oval shape of her face, while the top of her coiffure, her hairline, her eyebrows, and the lids of her eyes all repeat a single arc. The less sharp curve in the bottom of her eyes is echoed by her little smile. We are charmed by the result, but as much may not be said about the face of the infant. In young manhood as in old age, Stuart was inept at painting small children.

Mrs. Lopez and her son, Joshua is full of solecisms and inconsistencies, yet it is made by design and color into a charming picture. Conviction is manifest in every brushstroke. Refusing to accept the easy formulas of his master, Stuart has set out like David, with his pebble clutched in his slingshot, to topple the most gigantic problems of art.

Stuart's interest in giving a true description of the world as he saw it had made him immune to the fancier elements of the portraits he had encountered abroad. According to British custom, sitters should be placed in elegant surroundings which, by their very artificiality, showed that the subject was not an inhabitant of the ordinary world, but more rich, more noble, a being apart. When his Newport neighbors demanded that he execute a picture in this style, Stuart refused. Waterhouse tells us: "A committee of the Redwood Library, of Newport, waited upon him to engage him to paint a full-length of its generous founder, Abraham Redwood, then living next door to the painter, for which the young artist would have had a generous reward, but [despite] all that his parents and the rest of his friends could say, he declined it in sullen silence, and by so doing turned the popular tide in some degrees against him. . . . This occurrence cooled the zeal of many of his friends."

Stuart tried to keep his likenesses small and simple. Cosmo Alexander had painted Sir Alexander Grant— an aristocratic Scotchman on a visit to the family of his Newport daughter-in-law—standing at three-quarter length, a letter pouch in his hand. Two thirds of the background depicted paneling, broken into vertical segments, and serving to stop the space behind the figure. The other third opened up into a view of a marble balustrade beyond which extended a noble landscape. For his *John Bannister*, Stuart employed a similar composition, but removed the elegant details. He cut the figure off at the waist, amputating hips and legs and also the business of the hand with the pouch;

he carried the paneling across the entire picture, expunging the porch and the view. Nothing remains but the essential elements of the likeness itself.

Only once in his surviving Newport pictures did Stuart follow international tradition by adding a noble but irrelevant detail. He included in his portrait of a storekeeper's son, Robert Stoddard, Jr., a fluted column in the classical taste, but he crowded it over into a corner, and instead of painting the marble a conspicuous white, he gave it a greenish hue that blended in with the other colors. You have to look twice to make sure the shard of antiquity is really there.

The accessories Stuart wished to put in his pictures were the commonplace objects of every day. When he painted Francis and Saunders Malbone, the sons of another merchant, he tried to show them exactly as they appeared when engaged in their studies. The pie-crust table between them is a portrait, and a most ordinary inkstand is rendered with the passionate fidelity of a minor Dutch artist.

This picture, the most elaborate of Stuart's early works, reveals superlative promise. It does not seem to be a flat canvas cunningly marked to give a pretense of depth, but rather an actual cube of space. The eye is able to travel around the backs of the heads, to feel shapes and distances. Any art student could point out a dozen conventional mistakes of drawing, perspective, and design; but this picture might well make a student realize the limitations of formulas. Reality is not drawn here but communicated; we see, even if only dimly, the truth more powerful than truth itself.

Stuart studied anatomy by paying "a strong-muscle blacksmith" fifty cents an evening to pose. Convinced that his solitary war with the problems of art was going well, he felt no need for outside instruction or inspiration. Although boats plied perpetually from Newport to Boston, he made no effort to visit John Singleton Copley, America's leading painter, who was creating great portraits in an extension of the primitive realistic style Stuart practiced.

At Philadelphia, Charles Willson Peale, recently returned from studying painting in London, was applying new sophistication to the lyrical manner he had developed in the Colonial South. Peale recalled that in the 1770's he was approached—it was probably by Joseph Anthony—to accept as a pupil a young man whom he later inferred must have been Stuart. The mature artist was willing; the beginner was not.

Stuart's portrait of Waterhouse, painted in January 1775, shows a great development in his style, particularly in the achievement of likeness. The young experimenter had half escaped from the primitive limitations that had forced him to show faces as designs. Although the astringent quality is still there in the shaping of the head, the features are naturalistic. We should recognize Waterhouse if we met him on the street.

How much further Stuart, if left alone, would have carried his self-evolved style it is impossible to know, for the revolutionary agitation intervened. Incidents were multiplying; clearly there would soon be war. Like most Episcopalians a Tory, the painter's father determined to flee to some lands in Nova Scotia which he had bought at the time he gave up his partnership with Moffatt. His wife and daughter would stay behind until the millwright had tried the experiment of farming in a wild and distant province which he had never seen. But what of his son, now twenty years old? The social confusion was putting an end to all business for painters.

Years later, Stuart stated that he had disagreed with his father's politics, that he had wanted to enlist in the patriot army and fight the British. His horrified elder urged him to sail instead to London. Waterhouse had already gone there to study medicine, leaving Stuart no companion with whom to dispute about painting and music; Joseph Anthony and some of his wealthy patrons were willing to lend him passage money; he could not refuse this opportunity to seek a larger arena in which to practice his art.

Once he had made up his mind, he felt gay. He spent his last night in Newport playing the flute under the window of a young lady and mocking the nightcapped burghers who shouted for quiet from the neighboring windows. Then he went to British-held Boston to wait for his boat. During his short stay there, he gave instruction to a young boy who was himself to have a brilliant career in England as a painter. Mather Brown wrote to his aunts in 1817 that Stuart "was the first person who learnt me to draw at about twelve years of age at Boston. He lived then near Mr. Whiting's, a print-seller near Mill Bridge." In a year or so Brown was to run away from his grand-father and wander with a knapsack on his back through the countryside in a successful effort to make enough money as an itinerant painter of miniatures to follow his instructor to London.

During June or July 1775, at about the time of the Battle of Bunker Hill, Stuart left behind him his em-battled homeland. He had set out for the British Isles before, in the company of a distinguished and power-ful patron, but the result had been tragedy. Now he was alone, with only enough money in his pocket to keep him a few weeks in the British capital. He had but one letter of introduction, to Alexander Grant, the Scotch aristocrat with Newport connections whom Cosmo Alexander had painted. He relied principally on the chance that Waterhouse, from whom he had received no word, would be in London.

CHAPTER THREE
BATTLE FOR UNIQUENESS

WHEN Stuart reached London about November 1775, he hurried at once to the most recent address he had for Waterhouse. His friend, he was told, was attending medical school in Edinburgh. He stood dazed in the hallway before he returned to the street; his prospects had sunk to almost nothing. He took a tiny, airless room in the house of a tailor—probably John Palmer—in York Buildings, Buckingham Street, Strand, and ate as little as he could. Yet the few shillings in his pocket decreased daily.

Again he walked the pavements of a strange city with the gait that he remembered, the aimless shuffling of the dispossessed who have no place to go and no reason to walk except that they cannot always stand still. He spent a few pence on postage to Edinburgh and wrote Waterhouse a brokenhearted letter. "Your father," he remembered wistfully, "was at our house just before I left home, when he said Gilbert and Ben are so knit together like David and Jonathan, that if you heard from one, you would also hear from the other." A sentence in a later letter epitomizes Stuart's lonely state: "I don't know the day of the month or even what month, and I have no one to ask at present, but the day of the week is Tuesday, I believe."

Finally there was no more money to pay the land-lord or the baker; Stuart spent almost all his time on the streets now, afraid to return to his lodgings for fear he would be dispossessed. His daughter tells us that years later, when he was famous, "if any young man apparently not in very good circumstances came to him for instruction, it never failed to depress Stuart greatly, as his own early struggles were thus recalled."

Shuffling down Foster Lane one melancholy day, Stuart heard the notes of an organ radiating from a church, and his heart-quickened a little. His footsteps had a sudden purposeful ring as he hurried toward the door, but when he was about to enter, he remembered the pew woman; she would want her fee. He stood listening on the church steps like a hungry waif sniffling the odors outside the door of a pastry shop. Respectable people walked by him into the house of worship. The ragged young man, who had been so bold a few months before, watched them in an agony of hesitation for a long time before he dared ask what was going on within. He was told that the vestry was holding a competition for the position of organist.

Stuart trembled with excitement; he could play the organ, and in America he had been thought to play it well. If only he could get the position, it would mean meat and wine and other half-forgotten things. But when he looked at his rags, he realized that no vestry would ever give him a chance. He stood on the steps disconsolate, and the music cheered him no longer.

Then, with a sudden resolution, he hurried into the church, his head held high: a quick maneuver enabled him to avoid the pew woman and find a seat near the judges. One after another the spotless and somberly dressed contestants walked up to the organ, and as their notes echoed through the vault Stuart's spirits rose, for he knew he could do better. Studying the vestrymen with the knowledge of physiognomy that was later to make him famous, he selected the one with the most tolerant face and asked if a stranger might try his skill. Smiling at the ragged apparition, the man agreed. Thus Stuart found his way to the organ, and his fingers moved on the keys with all the ·eloquence of hunger and despair. He got the job and a salary of thirty pounds a year.

When Waterhouse returned to London the following summer, he found Stuart still lodging at the tailor's, still poor, and still struggling to get started as a painter. He had one canvas on his easel, a family group for Alexander Grant, the gentleman to whom he had a letter of introduction. Grant, Waterhouse tells us, "had paid him for it in advance. It remained long in his lodgings, and I am not sure that it ever was finished."

Waterhouse was horrified to discover that Stuart had sent no word to his family since they had parted

in Newport more than a year before. All his life the
painter suffered from a major block against writing letters; he was, Waterhouse remembered, "strongly attached to his parents"; his silence did not mean that
he was callous to their plight caught at home in the
jaws of civil war.

During the summer of 1775, Gilbert Stuart, Sr.,
had sailed to Nova Scotia, but by the time he had
cleared a few acres of farmland and raised a roof to go
over his wife's and daughter's heads, the wife and
daughter were trapped in Newport by a law forbid-
ding the emigration of Tories. Mrs. Stuart petitioned
the General Assembly of Rhode Island for a special
act that would enable them to leave. The act was
passed in February 1776, but permitted them to take
only "the wearing apparel and household furniture of
the family, and necessary provisions for the voyage."
Whatever assets the Stuarts had gathered in Newport
were no more.

Since Joseph Anthony had fled from his counting-
house to the safer retirement of a Pennsylvania farm,
Stuart could expect no backing from home—but
Waterhouse was the happy possessor of prosperous
English relations. What better fortune could there be
for a medical student than to have for an uncle the
rich practitioner and famous Quaker philanthropist
Dr. John Fothergill? When Fothergill arranged for
him to "walk" St. Thomas's and Guy's hospitals, Wa-

terhouse took convenient lodgings, and, so that Stuart
would not be living across the city, persuaded two of
Fothergill's nieces to put his friend up alternately in
their houses on Gracechurch Street: Mrs. James Free-
man received him at Number 39, Mrs. John Chorley
at Number 30. Both married to dry-goods merchants
of eminent respectability, they possessed the typical
Quaker distrust of art, yet Stuart now had safe roofs
over his head and clean linen in which to face the
world.

Fothergill, who had graduated from his prejudices
to be somewhat of a connoisseur, offered Stuart ten
guineas for a portrait of Waterhouse. Here was a subject Stuart had painted successfully in the Colonies;
hanging in a parlor so many leading Londoners visited, his new canvas would undoubtedly start him on
the road to fame. He dashed off a likeness in his best
Newport style and carried it triumphantly to his patron. That Fothergill indulged in no raptures was dis-
appointing, but could be explained away as British or
Quaker reserve. When Stuart called again to see how
the picture had been hung, it was nowhere in view,
nor could Stuart discover that it ever graced even a
bedroom wall. According to Waterhouse, Fothergill's
commission had been "a tactful way of giving him ten
guineas."

Having come to London not as a student seeking
knowledge but as a professional seeking conquest,

Stuart had attended no art schools, sat at the feet of no master. Thus, he behaved in an opposite manner from John Singleton Copley, who had also been dislodged by the Revolution. Although Copley had carried the American vernacular tradition to its highest flowering, although he had sent from Boston to London exhibitions paintings that were highly praised, when he set foot in Europe he placed all his great energies behind the effort to learn a newer, more knowing style. Following in the footsteps of almost every American artistic emigrant of his generation, Copley hurried to the studio of Benjamin West, a Pennsylvania expatriate who was court painter to George III.

West's early career had been very like Stuart's. He had started to draw almost spontaneously, amazing his Colonial neighbors, and while yet in his teens he had become a professional portraitist, practicing a self-taught style that made him a great success first in Lancaster, Pennsylvania, and then in the metropolis of Philadelphia itself. When a subscription had been taken up to send him to Italy, he had been the same age as Stuart was now. Although West's first view of the pictures he had read about in books left him disappointed, he never doubted that it was his duty to use them as the foundations of a rebuilt style. Soon the connoisseurs of Rome were calling him "the American Raphael." In 1763 he took a coach for England.

London frowned on the Colonial only a moment.

The Archbishop of York became his patron, and
then the King himself. Abandoning portrait-painting
as too menial a pursuit, he created vast story-telling
canvases, bringing to England the neo-classical movement that was soon to catch fire in France and produce
such artists as David. Many connoisseurs considered
West the painter most likely to revive the glories of the
Renaissance.

He took his mission with the unselfconscious seri-
ousness of his Quaker upbringing. It would have been
madness to bury in provincial Pennsylvania the great
international career that lay before him, but he never
forgot that his opportunity had been given him by the
citizens of that province. If he could not in person
bring painting to his homeland, his pupils would do
so. His studio became the first and perhaps the most
influential of all American art schools. Within its halls,
one Colonial after another emerged from his home-
spun style into the fine feathers of world art.

Stuart must have been familiar with West's reputation. He must have known that Charles Willson
Peale, who had been recommended to him as a teacher
in America, was a pupil of West's. Probably he had
heard that in order to be taken into the studio of the
powerful expatriate, all an American need do was
present himself and mention his origin. When Waterhouse returned, Stuart had an even closer link with
West's studio, for Waterhouse had presented letters of

introduction that enabled him to visit there. But Stuart did not feel he had anything to learn from West.

Stuart was trying to preserve his personal integrity by closing his ears to the critical opinions of all European connoisseurs, his eyes to the sophisticated glories of world art. In London there lived a genius who came as close as any man can to developing a purely individual style, but William Blake was a half-mad mystic, able to feed endlessly on the nectar of his own imagination. Stuart was not a mystic or tremendously concerned with imagination. His personal struggle was not to leave the world behind him in a rush of dream, but to show it as it was. The development of his Newport style had been increasingly toward realism.

In his earlier years, the exterior influences that had impinged upon him had been feeble: black-and-white engravings, poor versions of old masters, Cosmo Alexander's superficial, structureless work. Another artist might have learned much even from these, as Copley had from sources hardly more profound, yet the self-willed Stuart decided that it was wiser to rely on personal experimentation, and the result had satisfied the Newport connoisseurs.

In London it was less easy to ignore pressures from outside. His combination of pride, stubbornness, and poverty seems to have kept him to himself until Waterhouse joined him, but then the two friends set out to

explore. On a pocket map they marked with red pencil each street through which they walked, hoping to
cover the whole city. As a guidebook they used William Maitland's *The History of London from Its
Foundation to the Present Time.* The two huge volumes took up the city parish by parish, describing the
history of every old building in terms both erudite and
picturesque. The author had a dry common sense
most appealing to Americans. Thus, he doubted that
at the entertainment given in Westminster Palace by
Henry III for the marriage of his brother in 1243 the
number of dishes "amounted to 30,000. If we admit
the dishes to each have been a foot in diameter, the
present hall, which is bigger than that at the time of
Henry III, would exclusive of company only contain
15,048 dishes."

The painter's explorations called forcibly to his attention such a long past, in which tradition had a profound significance, as was unknown in America. Even
more disturbing to his confidence in his own untaught
artistic experimentation was his contact with great art.
"Stuart and I," Waterhouse wrote, "agreed to devote
one day a week to viewing pictures, wherever we
could get admittance. . . . We found nothing to
equal the collection at Queen's Palace or Buckingham
House." Among the many old masters which hung on
these walls, Americans were commonly most impressed by Raphael's cartoons at the Queen's Palace.

Stuart did not wish to be impressed, yet how could he deny that the pictures, although in so many ways contrary to his home-grown style, achieved marvelously what he himself wished to achieve: the realistic recording of visual truth.

So great was the momentum of Stuart's pride that he was unable to act upon this discovery. Instead of rushing to West's studio—there was a whole room given to West's paintings at the Queen's Palace—he tried hysterically to patch the crumbling walls that guarded his personal uniqueness. The principal result of Stuart's views of Old World art was to make it impossible for him to stick to his painting.

Instead, he threw himself into dissipation. Whenever he had money in his pocket, he spent it instantly in some wild spree. How grandly he treated his gay companions! As he carelessly tossed pound notes on the bar, he smiled to think that no one could guess he ever had been poor. After his money was gone he borrowed, and when he found he could not pay he threw himself into a depression as extreme as his high spirits had been. "With Stuart," Waterhouse remembers, "it was either high tide or low tide. In London he would sometimes lie abed for weeks, waiting for the tide to lead him on to fortune." But when at last a knocking on the door aroused the slovenly lad from his slovenly bed, it was not opportunity that knocked; it was the bailiff come to hustle him off to debtor's prison. Waterhouse often rescued him from sponging-houses by paying the demands for which he was confined. "Of my allowance of pocket money, he had two thirds, and more than once the other third."

Fothergill, an enthusiastic supporter of American liberties, felt guilty because England was engaged in a war to suppress those liberties: he backed his nephew's efforts to help the young American painter. Dr. William Curtis, author of *Flora Londinensis*, was persuaded to sit for his portrait. This picture may possibly have been finished, but when it was arranged that as a splashy exhibition piece for the Royal Academy Stuart should paint a full-length of Dr. John Coakley Lettsom, a fashionable practitioner who had been Fothergill's protégé, Stuart got entangled and soon gave up.

The appearance in his studio of two handsome sisters, one with dark hair and the other with reddish hair and blue eyes, inspired the young painter to attempt an act of gallantry that would put him more in line with fashionable London practice: he would paint one as the tragic, the other as the comic muse. This metaphoric approach required for success painting techniques entirely different from those Stuart possessed. The young ladies could hardly have been charmed with the result, that is if there was any result beyond a few flirtatious sittings.

Desperate to help his friend, Waterhouse took up among his fellow medical students a subscription to pay for an engraving of a popular professor; he engaged Stuart to make the painting. Stuart spent the money in a burst of hope and joy, but when the time came to get to work, he could not even make himself begin. Thus, he alienated the only friends he had in London. Fothergill, who felt obliged to pay back the money, refused to speak to Stuart again, and Waterhouse suffered, as he wrote, "inexpressible unhappiness and mortification, which at length brought on me a fever, the only dangerous disease I ever encountered."

Finally, so we read between the lines, Waterhouse completely lost patience, and the linen-draper Chorley, with whom Stuart was currently lodging, gave him to understand that he had outstayed his welcome. Faced with destitution once more, Stuart was forced to face something even more frightening: the state of his own intelligence. At last he realized that he had lost his battle to become a great painter by his own unaided powers. Late in 1776 or early in 1777 he gave in to the expedient he had spurned so long: he wrote to Benjamin West. His mood was abject misery. If he were to touch the mire, the pathologically proud young man must wallow in it to the lowest point of self-abasement:

Sir,

The benevolence of your disposition encourageth me, while my necessity urgeth me, to write you on so disagreeable a subject. I hope I have not offended by taking this liberty. My poverty and ignorance are my only excuse. Let me beg that I may not forfeit your good will, which to me is so desirable. Pity me, good sir. I've just arrived at the age of twenty-one, an age when most young men have done something worthy of notice, and find myself ignorant, without business or friends, without the necessities of life, so far that for some time I have been reduced to one miserable meal a day, and frequently not even that. Destitute of the means of acquiring knowledge, my hopes from home blasted, and incapable of returning thither, pitching headlong into misery, I have this only hope—I pray that it may not be too great—to live and learn without being a burden. Should Mr. West in his abundant kindness think of aught for me, I shall esteem it an obligation which shall bind me for ever with gratitude. With the greatest humility,

Sir, yours at command,

G. C. Stuart

CHAPTER FOUR

RING OUT THE OLD, RING IN THE NEW

ALTHOUGH Stuart had described himself as destitute, when he decided to follow up his letter to West with a personal visit he dressed himself as elegantly as his depleted wardrobe would allow. He had held on to at least one decent garment: a handsome coat. Having arranged his linen around it as best he could, he stepped into the street, starting on an errand that was to be portentous for American art.

He knocked on West's door at dinnertime. As luck would have it, among those inside was Joseph Wharton, a Tory merchant now in exile from Philadelphia but recently a close business associate of Joseph Anthony.

A servant, so Wharton remembered, came into the dining-room and handed West a slip of paper. Having read it, the painter said "I am engaged." Then, after a moment's hesitation: "Who is he?"

"He says he is an American."

At this information, West rose and walked into the anteroom where the mendicant waited. He must have been surprised to see not a ragged, hungry-looking creature, but "a handsome youth in a fashionable green coat." Furthermore, the intruder's face did not inspire confidence. It was thin and mobile, a little elfin-looking, with its sharp nose, narrow chin, and quick bright eyes. It was a clever face, perhaps a little too clever, the eyes not direct but shifty, the mouth rapid in speech but with a nervous tremble in silence. West could read plain on this striking countenance the marks of dissipation.

If Stuart matched his manner to his clothes, he was very grand, now that after more than a year of tribula-tion he had humiliated himself by appealing to the King's painter. He boasted of having swept Newport off its feet with his stunning portraits, handled his snuffbox with an air, and mentioned some great names. Since West had left America in 1760, he was unable to judge the young man's veracity; he listened with increasing doubt. Was this strange visitor really a painter; had he ever met the people of whom he spoke?

Excusing himself, West returned to his guests and said to Wharton: "There is a young man in the next room who says he is known in our city. Go you and see what you can make of him."

Wharton, who suspected that his benevolent host was easily put upon, was curt with the intruder. "You are known in Philadelphia?"

"Yes, sir."

"Your name is Stuart?"

"Yes."

"You have no letters for Mr. West?"

"No, sir."

"Whom do you know in Philadelphia?"

"Joseph Anthony is my uncle."

"That's enough—come in."

On the surface, it would seem that West and Stuart were fire and water, the eternal opposites. West lived quietly and happily within the moral preconceptions of his middle-class Quaker upbringing. All that was gay, elegant, evil in eighteenth-century London passed him by. He refused to paint countesses in the fine feathers of affluence; actresses and courtesans went to Reynolds's studio, not his. West believed that art demeaned itself when it reflected the lascivious passions of the pleasure-loving classes. His heroic compositions from ancient and modern history exemplified such qualities as filial piety or patriotism. Although George III, himself an enthusiastic family man, was moved, peers who believed that splendor should characterize a royal court commented sourly that West wended his way between his studio and Windsor Castle "with the staid look of one of the brethren going to and from chapel."

Seeing "a necessary connection between art and virtue," West, who considered himself the greatest of living painters, felt that he also had to be the most moral of men. He made fewer demands on others than on himself; tolerance was part of his code as well as generosity; and thus he befriended the wild-look-ing young man, as he befriended many another dissi-pated beginner. He found Stuart lodgings near his studio, at Number 27 on Villiers Street, a narrow lane of small houses running from the Strand to the muddy brink of the Thames (there was no embank-ment in those days). Undoubtedly West, in his ha-bitual manner, lent the new student a picture to copy, either one of his own works or an old master out of his extensive collection.

Shortly after Stuart had found a safe berth with West, his unstable hand betrayed him into dropping a valuable optical instrument; the camera lucida lay in fragments on the hearth. He stood with his back to the owner, waiting for the burst of anger with which he would himself have greeted such an accident. "Well, Stuart," West said mildly, "you may pick up the pieces." Years later, when one of Stuart's intimates compared West to a fool, Stuart gave way to fury: "I should prefer your playing practical jokes on others!" In 1816 his pupil Matthew Harris Jouett jotted down in his notebook that Stuart had said: "West [was] wiser than Reynolds, and was in fact as to goodness what Sir Joshua seemed. . . . By nature West was the wisest man he ever knew, but no Negro boy [was] more awkward in expressing his ideas. This came from want of literature."

West soon took Stuart on as an assistant, paying him a half-guinea a week for painting in draperies. Now, for the first time in his career, the young man worked not in lodgings but in what would today be called a studio! [1] To an elaborate house at 14 Newman Street, on the north side of Oxford Street, West had added a gallery terminating in two lofty rooms. The gallery was hung with West's sketches the whole way, except where casts of Venus and Apollo stood against one wall; the lofty rooms contained West's largest pictures, and usually the artist himself, soberly at work. Outside the windows was a garden which, with its arcade and statuary, had "an Italian look." The scene was so impressive that the servants walked on tiptoe, and visitors, even the greatest men of England, found themselves talking in whispers, as if at church.

Although he kept separate lodgings at least some of the time, Stuart soon used West's studio as his business address. His master, he remembered gratefully, came to treat him like a son. When John Trumbull, a student from Connecticut, appeared in July 1780, he found Stuart in possession of a private painting-room

[1] The word "studio" had not yet been imported from Italy. "Painting-room," the eighteenth-century term, reflects the fact that artists, with the exception of a few leading practitioners like West, worked in living-rooms, bedrooms, or barns without special architectural features.

close to West's. "He was dressed in an old black coat, with one half torn off the hip and pinned up, and looked more like a beggar than a painter."

If the quiet on Newman Street was shattered, Stuart was likely to be the cause. "I used very often to provoke my good master," he confessed, "though Heaven knows without intending it. You remember the color closet at the bottom of his painting-room. One day Trumbull and I came into his room and, little suspecting that he was within hearing, I began to lecture on his pictures, and particularly upon one then on his easel. I was a giddy, foolish fellow then. He had begun a portrait of a child, and he had a way of making curly hair by a flourish of his brush: thus, like a figure three.

" 'Here, Trumbull,' said I, 'do you want to learn how to paint hair? There it is, my boy! Our master figures out a head of hair like a sum in arithmetic. Let us see, we may tell how many guineas he is to have for this head by simple addition—three and three makes six, and three are nine, and three are twelve—'

"How much the sum would have amounted to, I can't tell, for just then in stalked the master, with palette knife and palette, and put to flight my calculations. 'Very well, Mr. Stuart,' said he—he always *mistered* me when he was angry, as a man's wife calls him *my dear* when she wishes him at the devil—'very well, Mr. Stuart; very well indeed!' You may believe that I looked foolish enough, and he gave me a pretty sharp lecture without my making any reply. When the head was finished, there were *no figures of three in the hair*."

Although Stuart found it necessary to make gestures of rebellion, he was fascinated by his new environment. The raw, ill-educated Colonial now met the first gentlemen of the realm. Too proud to accept social or cultural inferiority, he rapidly absorbed the breeding and culture of his associates. He startled Trumbull by stating: "Linnæus is right. Plato and Diogenes call man a biped without feathers—that's a shallow definition. Franklin's is better: 'a tool-making animal.' But Linnæus's is best: 'homo, animal *mendax, rapax, pugnax*.' "

Stuart amended his speech by imitating the elocution of the matinee idol John Kemble, who had become his friend. As he watched his manners blossom, he became prouder than ever. One day Dr. Johnson, with the immemorial condescension of Englishmen toward American pronunciation, asked Stuart where a Colonial such as he could have learned to speak so well. "Sir," replied Stuart, "I can better tell you where I did not learn it. It was not from your dictionary."

West's contribution to Stuart's art was the greatest and most difficult contribution a teacher can make. He did not attempt to drive the young man into painting as he himself painted. "Try it," he would say

when he made a suggestion, "and if it is not good you
can alter it." More often than not, Stuart did alter it.
In placing himself under West's tuition, he had admitted that he had much to learn from European art,
but he was far from surrendering his personal citadel.
Nor did West demand this surrender. He opened before Stuart's gaze a storehouse of technical wonders,
and urged his pupil to select only what he could use
for his own purposes.

Although Stuart was West's first assistant for four
or five years and often painted on his master's "ten-
acre canvases," he himself never attempted any of
those historical compositions which everyone who fre-
quented West's studio told him were the only high
form of art. "No one," he replied, "would paint history who could do a portrait," and he stuck to his own
specialty, the painting of faces, refusing the instruction
that would have enabled him to execute a complicated
picture.

Drawing in line was considered so basic to the art
of painting that the Royal Academy School taught
nothing else. West, who, like all American limners,
had started to paint before he knew how to draw, regarded this as overemphasis on a tool, yet he recognized that the tool was essential to historical painters.
According to Trumbull, West said one day to a
group of his students, Stuart included: "You ought to
go to the Academy and study drawing, but as you

would not like to go there without being able to draw
better than you do, if you will only attend, I will keep
a little academy and give you instruction every evening." Stuart came the first night, but soon got his
paper black all over. Losing patience, he stamped out,
and there is no record that he ever attended the Royal
Academy School. The famous painter Henry Fuseli
is reported to have said, on seeing one of Stuart's
drawings: "If this is the best you can do, you ought to
go and make shoes."

Stuart admitted in his old age that he had never
learned to do a line drawing, but insisted that such
knowledge was not an asset. Jouett made the following notes on one of his tirades: "Drawing the features
distinctly and carefully with chalk a loss of time. All
studies to be made with brush in hand. Nonsense to
think of perfecting oneself in drawing before one be-
gins to paint. . . . One reason why the Italians
never painted so well as other schools." He added
that when a line sketch is interposed between the crea-
tive mind and its vision of a completed picture, "a
fastidiousness ensues and, on the heels of that, dis-
appointment and disgust."

West's portrait style had little influence on Stuart,
for Stuart did not admire West's portraits. The older
man undertook likenesses only under pressure, and
then he employed conventional recipes. Well-born
English and Continental faces had been rounded and

colored by so many men for so many years that every brushstroke had learnt to fall into its place; highlights were placed exactly so; the middle tints had their accepted amount of brightness; the shadows their accepted amount of dark. The result was an image that looked as if it had been carved in the finest alabaster and then delicately polychromed.

One day in West's studio Stuart came on Trumbull painting a third student, William Dunlap. He was asked how he liked the picture. "Pretty well, pretty well, but more like our master's flesh than nature's. When Benny teaches the boys, he says: 'Yellow and white there,' and he makes a streak; 'red and white there,' and another streak; 'brown and red there for a warm shadow,' another streak; 'red and yellow there,' another streak. But nature does not color in streaks. Look at my hand; see how the colors are mottled and mingled, yet all is clear as silver."

Stuart, who had no aversion to exaggerating a story, told Dunlap an anecdote which, although inaccurate in detail, served to dramatize the difference between his portrait style and West's. The canvas involved was almost certainly not a likeness of George III, since Stuart seems never to have painted the King. Furthermore, West was Royal Historical Painter, not, as implied, the Royal Portrait-Painter entrusted with the manufacture of routine official likenesses.

"Mr. West treated me very cavalierly on one occasion," Stuart stated, "but I had my revenge. It was the custom whenever a new Governor General was sent out to India that he should be complimented by a present of His Majesty's portrait, and Mr. West, being the King's painter, was called upon on all such occasions. So, when Lord —— was about to sail for his government, the usual order was received for His Majesty's likeness. My old master, who was busily employed upon one of his ten-acre pictures in company with prophets and apostles, thought he would turn over the King to me. He never could paint a portrait.

" 'Stuart,' said he, 'it is a pity to make His Majesty sit again for his picture: there is the portrait of him that you painted; let me have it for Lord ——. I will retouch it, and it will do well enough.'

"*Well enough!* Very pretty! thought I. You might be civil when you ask a favor. So I *thought*, but I *said:* 'Very well, sir.' So the picture was carried down to his room, and at it he went. I saw he was puzzled. He worked at it all that day. The next morning, 'Stuart,' said he, 'have you got your palette set?'

" 'Yes, sir.'

" 'Well, you can soon set another. Let me have the one you prepared for yourself. I can't satisfy myself with that head.'

"I gave him my palette and he worked the greater part of that day. In the afternoon I went up into his room, and he was hard at it. I saw that he had got up to the knees in mud. 'Stuart,' says he, 'I don't know how it is, but you have a way of managing your tints unlike everybody else. Here; take the palette, and finish the head.'

" 'I can't, sir.'

" 'You can't?'

" 'I can't indeed, sir, as it is, but let it stand till to-morrow morning and get dry, and I will go over it with all my heart.'

"The picture was to go away the day after the morrow, so he made me promise to do it early next morning. You know, he never came down into the painting-room at the bottom of the gallery until about ten o'clock. I went into his room bright and early, and by half past nine I had finished the head. That done, Rafe [West's son Raphael] and I began to fence, I with my maulstick and he with his father's. I had just driven Rafe up to the wall, with his back to one of his father's best pictures, when the old gentleman, as neat as a lad of wax, with his hair powdered, his white silk stockings, and yellow morocco slippers, popped into the room, looking as if he had stepped out of a bandbox. We had made so much noise that we did not hear him come down the gallery or open the door. 'There, you dog,' says I to Rafe, 'there I have you! And nothing but your background relieves you.'

"The old gentleman could not help smiling at my

technical joke, but soon looking very stern, 'Mr. Stu-art,' said he, 'is this the way you use me?'

" 'Why, what's the matter, sir? I have neither hurt the boy nor the background.'

" 'Sir, when you knew I had promised that the pic-ture of His Majesty should be finished today, ready to be sent away tomorrow, thus to be neglecting me and your promise! How can you answer it to me or to yourself?'

" 'Sir,' said I, 'do not condemn me without exam-ining the easel. I have finished the picture; please to look at it.' He did so; complimented me highly; and I had ample revenge for his 'It will do well enough.' "

Stuart loved to feel that he was on his own, breast-ing by himself the waves of destiny. On a visit to the Royal Academy School, he heard the aspirants, who were drawing from the antique as he refused to do, name the old masters they wished to imitate; one would like to paint like Rembrandt; another visual-ized himself as Titian; while a third would follow in the steps of "the gentle but divine Raphael." Finally Stuart interposed, remarking that probably he was a base fellow of low taste, but that his only interest was in copying what he saw before him. "I will not follow any master. I wish to find out what nature is for my-self, to see her with my own eyes." He was preening himself on the originality of these sentiments when he felt a hand upon his shoulder. Behind him stood the great academician Gainsborough. "That's right, my lad," Gainsborough said. "Adhere to that, and you will be a great artist."

When as a young man in Newport Stuart had repudiated stilted mannerisms and artificial conventions, he had believed himself highly original, yet a similar revolt was welling up at hundreds of places in hundreds of breasts. Gainsborough had passed through it, thousands of miles away from Stuart and a half-generation before. A modified naturalism had battered its way even into the highest ranks of British court painting. People were still shown as noble and handsome, but they no longer inhabited a special, sealed world of birth and elegance. Countesses were healthy young girls who walked in gardens and picked flowers. Earls stepped from throne rooms to the quarter-decks of boats; instead of fingering lace, they rested strong hands on cannon.

The old stereotypes had given painter and sitter little choice in the creation of likenesses. Both knew how an aristocrat should look; the only requirement was a brilliant application of a formula. But the new ideal, which attempted to show the sitter as an individual, brought with it a conflict. If the society belle was beautiful of face and refined of manner, everything was easy; you just put her down as she was. But supposing she was ugly and clumsy; what were you to do then? The artist was supposed to achieve the impossible: he was both to create a true likeness and gloss over the unflattering truth.

The successful British artist John Hoppner told one of his pupils that "in painting ladies' portraits, he used to make as beautiful a face as he could, then give it a likeness to his sitter, working down from the beautiful state till a bystander should cry out: 'Oh, I see a likeness coming!' Whereupon he stopped, never venturing to make it more like."

By mocking the method which society forced upon him, Hoppner was expressing distaste. Battle lines were beginning to be drawn which, when they became clearer, were to end in the destruction of the portrait as a major activity of major artists. Benjamin West, often a leader in esthetic evolution, characterized likenesses as "mawkish and wearisome monotonies"; he refused to spend "anxious, laborious hours in becoming a fashionable painter of vacant faces."

The two men who were to break down England's preoccupation with likenesses—Constable and Turner—were already born when Stuart stepped on the London scene, but the portrait was still king. All artists working in this mode were facing within themselves the problem that Stuart faced: how to be true to nature and their own vision, and yet sell their work. In the canvases of every important portraitist we find a veering between the downright and the socially smart, the sincere and the salable.

Whether he was conscious of it or not, Stuart's reactions were part of the movement of the times. Looking round from the vantage-point of West's studio, he discovered much in the painting of his contemporaries which fitted his own individual needs. His work evolved in the directions of the most up-to-date English styles.

In 1777, after he had been with West less than twelve months, Stuart emerged as a professional. He exhibited *A Portrait of a Gentleman* at the Royal Academy, where it attracted no notice whatsoever. The next year he exhibited nothing, although he executed the impressive self-portrait which is the earliest surviving example of his English style. In their own likenesses, artists can give completer expression to their aspirations than in commercial pictures, which must satisfy a paymaster. It is of particular interest to see how Stuart worked when he had to please no one but himself.

As compared with his *Benjamin Waterhouse*, painted in Newport three years before, the self-portrait reveals greatly increased technical skill. The early image was crudely composed. Although Stuart's interest had been in the face, the body, arm, and books were not adequately subordinated; they confused the picture. But in the self-portrait Stuart has made knowing use of chiaroscuro to place the features in a strong light and all other parts of the composition in shadow.

Color complements this emphasis. The face is brightly tinted, but the large "Rubens hat" is black, and the dark-brown coat merges with the dark-brown background. Accessories are no longer accurately defined objects, but rather semi-abstract elements of composition that serve to make rational the off-center placing of the head. Hard and limited by sharp outlines, Waterhouse's features seem to have been carved, with aching attention, from some unyielding substance. In the self-portrait, however, the shapes are fluently rendered. They are alive, active, vital.

On the surface, everything seems changed, but underneath Stuart is still the same man. His battle had always been to show undiluted the truth as he saw it, and his Newport evolution had carried him increasingly toward emphasis on the truth of character. The self-portrait shows him still on the same road. Far from being prettified or noble, the likeness is a passionate attempt to dig deep into psychological verity. We see personified on canvas the wild career we have been following. Stuart shows himself as a brash, dissatisfied, and self-centered young man, brilliant with an unhealthy brilliance. The picture is almost frightening in the deep self-understanding it reveals; as if the young man were not only conscious of the cankers in his spirit, but actually proud of them.

A year later, in 1779, he exhibited at the Royal Academy a picture which seems to have been inspired

by a desire to attract attention. A young boy, J. Ward,
is depicted in a costume from the time of Van Dyck.
But Stuart's excursion into the past did not extend beyond subject matter; the technique is definitely contemporary. Indeed, there is quite a startling resemblance to Gainsborough, whose "dragging method of
tinting" Stuart praised as an old man. A charming tour
de force, the canvas is in sharp contrast with the self-
portrait. It shows the artist, probably under advice
from West, trying to escape from his basic realism to a
more decorative style. When the picture created no
stir, Stuart gave up such experiments, as far as we
know forever. The next pictures we have from his
brush vary from the norm of British portraiture by
being harder, dryer, more downright. Stuart's commercial likenesses remained for some years less fluent
and more conventional than his self-portrait had been.

In 1781 his work began to attract notice. The
critic of the *St. James Chronicle* regarded Stuart's
Benjamin West as the equal of any portrait in the
Royal Academy show. This was high praise, as there
were twelve canvases by Reynolds and a full-length
by Gainsborough. Enchanted, Stuart spent hours before the picture. When West found him there, he
said "You have done well, Stuart, very well. Now all
you have to do is to go home and do better."

Stuart soon became sufficiently well known to inspire detractors. One critic wrote: "Mr. Stuart is in

partnership with Mr. West, where it is not uncommon for wits to divert themselves with applications for things they do not immediately want because they are told by Mr. West that Mr. Stuart is the only portrait-painter in the world; and by Mr. Stuart that no man has any pretensions in history-painting but Mr. West. After such authority, what can we say of Mr. Stuart's painting?"

It was whispered that Stuart "made a tolerable likeness of the face, but as to the figure he could not get below the fifth button." Perhaps to overcome such criticism he agreed to do a full-length of a Scotch gentleman, William Grant of Congalton. However, he was delighted to put off the first sitting when Grant remarked that the day was more suited to ice-skating than to standing for one's portrait. Stuart was an expert skater by English standards; he told a friend that his "celerity and activity accordingly attracted crowds on the Serpentine," but when a crack developed in the ice, he was forced to return with his sitter to the studio. Suddenly Stuart had an inspiration; he decided to paint Grant in the attitude of skating, "with the appendage of a winter scene in the background." After the picture was almost completed, Joseph Baretti, the famous Italian lexicographer, called on West and, seeing the canvas in a corner, cried "Who but the great artist West could have painted such a one!" On a subsequent visit he found Stuart at work on the portrait.

"What, young man, does Mr. West permit you to touch his pictures?" When Stuart replied that the painting was altogether his own, Baretti frowned sagely and remarked: "Why, it is almost as good as Mr. West can paint."

In later years Stuart told many anecdotes, not all of them credible, to demonstrate how he was "suddenly lifted into fame" by this one picture. It is hard to believe that when Stuart was in Reynolds's studio, the Duke of Rutland rushed in and shouted excitedly to the President of the Royal Academy, who undoubtedly had already visited the show for which he was responsible: "I wish you to go with me to the exhibition. There is a portrait there you ought to see. Everyone is enchanted with it." Reynolds, so Stuart continued, asked who had painted it. "A young man named Stuart." The tale ends with Stuart, suffused in blushes, making modestly for the door.

The newspapers, although filled with gossip about the exhibition, do not back up Stuart's story that Grant went there dressed in the skating-costume Stuart had painted: "The crowd followed him so closely that he was compelled to make his retreat, for everyone was exclaiming: 'That is he! That is the gentleman!' " Stuart asserted that he himself had to stay away lest he be stifled with praise.

As usual, he had embellished what was fundamentally fact: the painting did attract much attention.

Thus Sir John Collum, the antiquary and divine who was one of the most popular men of learning in London, wrote a friend: "One would have thought that almost every attitude of a single picture had long been exhausted in this land of portrait-painting, but one is now exhibited which I recollect not before—it is that of skating. There is a noble portrait, large as life, thus exhibited, which produces the most powerful effect."

The best comment on the relationship between Stuart's style and that of his London contemporaries is supplied by the adventures of the picture when, after a century of obscurity, it was rescued from a domestic wall and returned to the scene of its former triumph. Shown in 1878 at a Royal Academy exhibition of old masters, the canvas looked much the same; the major metamorphosis was on the label. It was attributed to Gainsborough.

As Whitley has pointed out, this attribution bothered the critics. They all agreed that the landscape background had much in common with Gainsborough, but they were puzzled by the likeness. The *Daily Telegraph*'s critic suggested Romney, but his colleague on the *Times* replied that Romney never painted a "figure like this for force, ease of movement, and fine yet bold execution." He preferred Hoppner or Raeburn. Raeburn got the votes of the *Illustrated London News* and the *Art Journal*, the latter paper adding: "A more graceful and manly figure was surely never painted by an English artist, and if Gainsborough were that artist, this is unquestionably his masterpiece."

Stuart's success at the Royal Academy show of 1782 inspired him to establish an independent studio. "Today the exhibition closes . . . ," Mrs. Hoppner wrote on June 3. "Stuart has taken a house, I am told, of £150 rent in Berners Street, and is going to set up as a great man." Although, as a matter of fact, Stuart only moved a few doors from West's studio, to 7 Newman Street, it was a major move. He was now on his own.

CHAPTER FIVE

PERSONAL FAILURES AND
PROFESSIONAL TRIUMPHS

WITHIN two years after he had set up for himself, Stuart was famous; Dunlap remembers that he "had his
full share of the best business in London, and prices
equal to any except Sir Joshua Reynolds and Gainsborough." In November 1784, William Temple
Franklin wrote to his grandfather, Benjamin Franklin, that Stuart "is esteemed by West and everybody
the first portrait-painter now living; he is, moreover,
an American. I have seen several of his performances
which seem to me very great indeed. He is astonish-
ing for likenesses. I hear West says that 'he nails the
face to the canvas.'" In 1787 the critic of the *World*
called Stuart "the Van Dyck of the time" and insisted that Gainsborough's work "shrinks and fades
away" when compared to Stuart's. Some connoisseurs
prophesied that he would become the leading portrait-
painter in England; Reynolds, Romney, and Gainsborough were coming to the end of their careers, while
the new generation of English-born painters—Lawrence, Beechey, Hoppner, and Raeburn—had not
yet risen to great prominence.

Here was an amazing metamorphosis. Less than
ten years before, Stuart had been a crude Colonial art-

ist no longer able to finish a picture; now he was a leader in one of the most sophisticated schools of portrait-painters ever known. And worldly prosperity followed Stuart's fame. He lifted his price for a head from five guineas to thirty, and, in 1785, moved to a splendid house on fashionable New Burlington Street, off Regent Street, for which he paid one hundred guineas a year. He imitated West by setting up, in some of the rooms, a perpetual exhibition of his own work.

The painter, who was just turning thirty, was beside himself with delight. Sometimes he saw in his mind's eye a ragged vagabond shuffling past closed doors, staring dully at the dandies in their fine carriages; and then he felt that this vision must be exorcised at any cost. When he remembered how he had starved on the streets of London, he shook his head angrily and hired the best French cook money could buy. In his dress, Dunlap tells us, "he emulated in style and costliness the leader of English fashion, the Prince of Wales. . . . He lived in splendor and was the gayest of the gay. As he said of himself, he was a great beau." He was soon earning fifteen hundred pounds a year, but he spent his huge income faster than it came in. The sponging-houses and the bailiffs' courts that had known him as a ragged boy saw him again as a fine gentleman. To extricate himself, he had to borrow money at exorbitant interest.

His family later defended his extravagance on the grounds that he needed, for business reasons, to impress the social world; but Reynolds and Gainsborough lived in no such style and moved in more exalted circles. Neither Stuart's manner nor his art appealed to the socially correct. His most fashionable patrons, like the upstart Duke of Northumberland, were men who thought of themselves as connoisseurs and gave employment to many artists. His work was particularly admired by such radicals as the Duke of Rutland and Colonel Isaac Barré, who had, in the Houses of Lords and Commons, supported the American cause.

If a peer graced Stuart's dinner table, he was usually a man of action who had earned his own title. The painter was friendly with the sea-dog George, Lord Rodney, and even more so with Admiral John Jervis, recently created Earl of St. Vincent. The diarist Joseph Farington later jotted down St. Vincent's complaint that "Stuart had received through his recommendation at least two thousand pounds, and that Stuart had behaved most ungratefully to him."

Stuart's closest intimates belonged to what would be called today "café society." He was often seen with the actor John Kemble, and was gallant to Mrs. Siddons. So as not to be out of place among "the best musicians of London," whom he assiduously cultivated, he took lessons in the flute from a German who played in the King's band.

William Thomas Parke, the principal oboe at the opera house, tells us that Stuart belonged to a club including "two or three other friends from the opera house" and William Shield, the vastly successful composer of ballad operas. Every Saturday night in the Haymarket "we supped after the play and the Italian opera were ended." When on one occasion Parke dined the next day at Stuart's, he joined "a large party," including a famous engraver and "a gentleman of fortune who was sitting to Stuart." Parke complained of a headache, and the painter convulsed the company with one of his famous puns: "If a man's head comes in contact with a club overnight, it may be expected that it will ache the next day."

Stuart, Parke remembered, "was a little enthusiastical or pretended to be so. Rising from his chair suddenly, [he] exclaimed to me with great vehemence: 'Sit still! Don't stir for your life!' I stared at him with astonishment, thinking he must be mad, till in a subdued tone he added: 'I beg your pardon, but your drapery as you now sit is very effective, and I wish to make a sketch of it before you move.' "

No one need be surprised that the young man who had lived on charity for years became with success overbearing and insolent. When his old disciple

Mather Brown came to call, Stuart showed himself at the window and then instructed his servant to say he was out. Listening over the stair well, Stuart heard Brown insist that he must be at home, since he had been at the window. "Yes, sir," the servant replied, "and he saw you, and he says he is not at home."

Stuart gleefully repeated this incident to his friends, whom he kept constantly amused by ridiculous anecdotes. Dunlap repeats one that was typical: "In the early period of Stuart's career as an independent portrait-painter, he had for his attendant a wild boy, the son of a poor widow, whose time was full as much taken up by play with another of the painter's household, a fine Newfoundland dog, as by attendance upon his master. The boy and dog were inseparable; and when Tom went on an errand, Towser must accompany him. Tom was a terrible truant, and played so many tricks that Stuart again and again threatened to turn him off, but as often Tom found some way to keep his hold on his eccentric master. One day, as story-tellers say, Tom stayed when sent on an errand until Stuart, out of patience, posted off to the boy's mother determined to dismiss him; but on his entering, the old woman *began first*. 'Oh, Mr. Stuart, Tom has been here!'

" 'So I supposed.'

" 'Oh, Mr. Stuart, the dog!'

" 'He has been here too. Well, well, he shall not come again; but Tom must come home to you. I will not keep him.'

" 'Oh, Mr. Stuart, it was the dog did it.'

" 'Did what?'

" 'Look, sir! Look here! The dog overset my mutton pie, broke the dish, greased the floor, and eat the mutton.'

" 'I'm glad of it. You encourage the boy to come here, and here I will send him.'

" 'It was the dog, sir, eat the mutton.'

" 'Well, the boy may come and eat your mutton. I dismiss him; I'll have no more to do with him.'

"The mother entreated; insisted it was the dog's fault; told over and again the story of the pie, until Stuart, no longer hearing her, conceived the plan of a trick upon Tom, with a prospect of a joke founded upon the dog's dinner of mutton pie. 'Well, well, say no more. Here's something for the pie and to buy a dish. I will try Tom again, provided you never let him know that I came here today, or that I learned from you anything of the dog and the pie.' The promise was given, of course, and Stuart hastened home as full of his anticipated trick to try Tom as any child with a new rattle. Tom found his master at his easel where he had left him, and was prepared with a story to account for his delay, in which neither his mother, nor Towser, nor the mutton made parts.

" 'Very well, sir,' said the painter. 'Bring in dinner. I shall know all about it by and by.' Stuart sat down to *his* mutton, and Towser took his place by his side as usual; while Tom, as usual, stood in attendance. 'Well, Towser, your mouth don't water for your share. Where have you been? Whisper.' And he put his ear to Towser's mouth, who wagged his tail in reply. 'I thought so. With Tom to his mother's?'

" 'Bow-wow.'

" 'And have you had your dinner?'

" 'Bow.'

" 'I thought so. What have you been eating? Put your mouth nearer, sir.'

" 'Bow-wow!'

" 'Mutton pie—very pretty—you and Tom have eaten Mrs. Jenkins's mutton pie, ha?'

" 'Bow-wow.'

" 'He lies, sir! [cried Tom]. I didn't touch it. He broke Mother's dish and eat all the mutton.'

"From that moment Tom thought if he wished to deceive his master, he must leave Towser at home, but rather on the whole concluded that what with the dog, the devil, and the painter, he had no chance of successful lying."

Concerning the illicit love affairs the tempestuous Stuart must have had, the record is, of course, silent; but we do know about Charlotte Coates. Shortly before he had set up for himself, he had increased his knowledge of anatomy by attending lectures given for medical students at the Windmill Street School by the learned, literary, and alcoholic Dr. William Cumberland Cruikshank. There he became so friendly with a fellow pupil, the son of Dr. William Coates (or Coats), that he visited his new friend's family at Reading, in Berkshire County. Stuart became popular with the father, a practicing physician, and all the children. He found particular comfort in playing the flute while fourteen-year-old Charlotte sang in fine contralto voice. It was such a gently innocent scene, there in the quiet of a provincial town, as his harried soul longed for.

However, the girl changed, with the amazing suddenness of her sex, into an "extremely pretty" young lady; her voice took on a disturbing richness that the superb musicianship which came naturally to her made strike directly at Stuart's heart. Relaxed friendship was no longer possible; he proposed marriage.

Charlotte was eager, deeply in love, but her family, although of no particular financial or social station, "opposed the match violently." Her father, as she remembered in later years, admired Stuart's "genius," yet was "perfectly aware of his reckless habits." Months of heart-rending negotiation had to be lived through before on May 10, 1786 the Rev. Mr. Springate of Reading married the painter, at the age of thirty, to his eighteen-year-old charmer.

If Stuart had promised to reform, the promise came to nothing. Now that he had a beautiful voice in the family, he gave huge parties at which his musical friends played. It was his joy to join them on the flute and hear his lady sing to their expert notes. Throughout a long life she looked back to these occasions as the apex of her existence. To her children she boasted that even the over-critical Fuseli made her repeat her songs.

Still the money went out faster than it came in. At one desperate time Stuart even took advantage of his beloved benefactor; he borrowed back from Mrs. West a portrait of her husband he had given her as a token of gratitude. He wanted, he explained, to touch up some rough place. Instead he sold the picture to Alderman Boydell. Probably he had meant to copy it for Boydell, but, having delayed too long, had at last sent the original in the confident belief that he would paint another for Mrs. West. He never got around to it.

What are we to make of Stuart's irresponsibility? His biographers have usually ducked the problem by denying that it exists. If Stuart, tossing off beakers of port in the Valhalla where dead artists go, can read what has been written about him, how often his ribald laugh must startle his gay and ghostly companions! He told his pupils that when painting a portrait "you cannot be too particular in what you do to see

what animal you are putting down." But most of Stuart's biographers have drawn a picture of him as full
of polite evasions as are those smirking society likenesses against which the great painter reacted. Such
aberrations as are considered correct for artists are
given him: he was, we are told, a poor businessman,
a little eccentric on the surface, but underneath as pure
as any new-born lamb. Snuff is permitted him, but not
liquor.

Writers who move in the never-never-land of polite biography must make such pious statements to
keep from walking the only other road open to them,
that of showing Stuart as a grinning devil, vicious because of an inherent love of evil. For this world of vir-
ginal, scholarly pretense is bound by the same alter-
natives as the *Godey's Lady's Book* of yesterday or
the soap operas of today's television. A man is either a
hero or a villain, altogether good or altogether bad.

Should we examine Stuart in the same mood of ob-
jective sympathy with which he examined his sitters,
we should see before us a creature hag-ridden by
jangling nerves. Toward the end of his London period he started a self-portrait as a present for his wife.
He only undertook the task after violent persuasion,
and he was unable to finish it. The sketched-in canvas
is one of the most anguished, tortured pictures this
writer has ever seen. The lean face is twisted with
passionate unhappiness.

Clearly Stuart's excesses were not the result of high spirits; he never found the world a restful lodging-house. The eighteenth-century citizen of Maryland, Andrew Ellicott, might have been thinking of Stuart when he wrote home after his first meeting with the Yankees that "these northern gentry appear mightily pestered with a restless and uneasy spirit which some good people who are now lodging with me suppose must proceed from the remains of that witchcraft which formerly prevailed in their country." But Stuart's witches, like every witch that bestrode a broomstick, rode it through the firmament of his own mind.

Almost a decade had passed since that awful moment when Stuart had appeared, an elegantly dressed beggar, on the doorstep of Benjamin West. Like a desperate man leaping from a bridge, he had thrown himself into the stream of world art that swept through the studio of the King's painter. The tides he had so dreaded carried him to prosperity and fame, yet again and again he tried to swim against the current.

Although Stuart remained intimate with West, he felt it necessary, as soon as he had set up a studio of his own, to demonstrate his independence in a public and dramatic manner. Anyone who knew anything about art in London was conscious that West was second only to Reynolds (whom he was to succeed as president) as a power in the Royal Academy. Indeed, it had been West's influence with the King which had

brought royal patronage to the more distinguished artists when, in 1768, they decided to form their own
academy in opposition to the Society of Artists, where
they were being outvoted by their mediocre brethren.

Stuart's works were welcomed at the Royal Academy, yet in 1783 he submitted nothing there. Instead, he sent nine canvases to the Society of Artists,
which had been staggering along as an outlet for the
second-rate. The members, who had not for years had
so important a recruit, were beside themselves for joy;
his pictures outshone everything else in the show; he
was instantly elected to the company of his inferiors;
but even his help did not keep the Society from falling
on such evil days that it could not hold another exhibition for many years.

In 1784 Gainsborough threatened to secede from
the Royal Academy because the members insisted on
adhering to their rule that pictures be hung on "the
line," eight and a half feet from the floor, although his
Three Princesses had been painted for a lower spot.
The *St. James Chronicle* reported that Stuart would
join Gainsborough in founding a rival organization.
However, the plan failed to mature, and in 1785,
the year Stuart moved to New Burlington Street, he
returned to the Royal Academy exhibition with three
portraits. This was the last time.

Once he had his private gallery well installed, he
relied on his ability to lure connoisseurs, patrons, and

newspaper paragraphers to his own house; he sent to
no public exhibitions. The Royal Academicians, who
regarded support of their organization, with its schools
and pension funds, as a professional duty, were annoyed, and the *Public Advertiser* asked whether Stuart was "already so giddy with the summit of his profession as to overlook what is expected of him? . . .
His head of Col. Barré would have counted largely in
the exhibition in the sum of money [from admissions]
and skill." Stuart had killed his chances of being
elected to the Royal Academy, an honor most artists
eagerly desired and considered a great help in selling
pictures.

By temperament, he was a revolutionary. Although
modern critics, more gifted with anachronistic prejudice than historical insight, have accused him of pro-
ducing typical society portraits, his own contemporaries attacked his work for lacking the expected
graces. In 1782 one newspaper stated that he "seldom
fails of a likeness, but wants freedom of pencil and elegance of taste." Another called his portrait of a Swed-
ish gentleman "a fine picture and a strong likeness,"
but added: "If we are not mistaken, the original would
not like to carry the copy of himself back to Sweden."

Year after year, the comments ran the same way.
His personages, it was charged, lacked "a distin-
guished air." In 1805, after Stuart had returned to
America, a critic thus summarized his London career:

"When we speak of him as the most accurate painter, we mean to say that, having a very correct eye, he gave the human figure exactly as he saw it, without any attempt to dignify or elevate the character; and was so exact in depicting its lineaments that one may almost say of him what Hogarth said of another artist, 'that he never deviates grace'; and from all of which we may fairly infer that he was never a favorite painter with the ladies."

A half-dozen of his surviving English portraits depict a man for every one depicting a woman, yet he could create a marvelous likeness of an adolescent girl, as his *Augusta Montagu* shows. We suspect that his emotions were deeply involved in this portrait, for behind the lyrical image lay one of the wildest and most publicized tragedies of eighteenth-century London.

Before Miss Montagu was born, the Celestial Fablist set the action in motion in a millinery shop. It was a hackneyed story at first: a beautiful salesgirl, a great lord twice her age smitten as he walked by on the street; passionate offers and discreet replies; temptations and blushes and at last surrender. But now, as the story gains momentum, strange elements enter. The Earl of Sandwich, that aging libertine, did not throw off Miss Martha Ray as he had thrown off so many others. Neither did he marry her, of course, but he took her to Hinchingbrooke, his family seat, and on to London when he became First Lord of the Admiralty.

Miss Ray was faithful to her Earl; gave him a large brood of children, of whom Augusta was one; behaved in a manner which was "all the most exacting could have required"; and charmed everyone with "the beauty of her singing and the modesty of her behavior."

The stage was now set for the entrance of a young man ten years her junior, Lieutenant James Hackman of the British army. He could not bear it that one so good and so beautiful as Miss Ray should be an old libertine's doxy; he offered to make an honest woman of her; he offered marriage. But she smiled sweetly and said that she was very happy.

Spiritualized, or so he thought, by his love, the young man tore the military red from his shoulders and replaced it with the black robes of the Church of England. As Vicar of Wiveton, he administered to the puling babies of the poor, but always there floated through his mind that vision. Now he spoke to the Earl's mistress of her soul, begging her to remember the hereafter, but the beautiful body that he could never quite ignore just smiled and waved its fan. After long meditation, he realized what he had to do. He followed her to the theater one winter night; he waited while she laughed at the scenes of *Love in a Village*; he saw her come out, her face flushed with the memory of pleasure; and then he shot her through the forehead. She died instantly, but the bullet he had saved for his own suicide failed. Lying on the pavement slightly wounded and covered with blood, he struck himself on the head repeatedly with the butt of his gun, but to no avail.

Society rocked with the scandal. It became the major topic of conversation at Dr. Johnson's club, where the great pundit quarreled with his intimates over the interpretation of the evidence. Since the war with America was on and the Earl was First Lord of the Admiralty, Horace Walpole wrote: "I do not doubt but it will be found that the assassin was a dissenter, and instigated by the Americans to give such a blow to the state." But the Vicar proved to be of unexampled piety and patriotism. Men speculated on his motivations and his emotions; women wept oceans in their sympathy for the fallen churchman. Inserting himself in the forefront of the sensation, Boswell rode with the murderer to the gallows and bade him a fond farewell under the shadow of the gibbet. All London had a wonderful time.

Somewhere in the background cowered a fourteen-year-old girl, Augusta Montagu, the dead woman's daughter. Already in an anomalous position, she was now marked for life. No one would ever meet her who did not recall her illegitimate birth and her flamboyant family tragedy. Stuart too must have known her history, but the likeness he painted of her expresses nothing but youth and gaiety and innocence.

Transmuted by the painter's brush, Augusta Montagu goes down to posterity as a symbol of unclouded young womanhood.

Perhaps Stuart saw in her a reflection of his own worldly plight. They were both gay, perhaps a little too gay. They walked the world like ordinary people, yet around them both were intangible bars not of their own making. Run as fast as they would, sit quietly as monk or nun, their prison was always round them. They might reach their hands through the crevices, touching lovers, touching friends, but they could never draw another human being really close. Two outcasts moved in the studio together: the rising painter, the budding girl. Stuart determined to paint out of both their lives the pain and the memory.

The portrait is the loosest and most lyrical of all Stuart's English works. The brush flew in his hands, putting on color lightly, surely, with an instantaneous rightness he was not to achieve again until much later in his career. The white cap with its blue trim sits jauntily on the honey-colored hair, while the down-ward-leaning face, smiling at a letter held in delicate hands, is infused with girlish joy, the pure radiance of a happy child hardly conscious that she is a woman. The eyes are put in with so light a stroke that they have a transparent glow. In contrast to the position of the head, the body leans back in a gesture that is full of life yet completely contained within the quadri-

lateral of the frame. Perhaps the most amazing technical triumph of this inspiration is the way everything
flows—no frill, or feature, or lock of hair is static—
and yet the viewer's eye finds itself at rest. Every
movement, every shape is balanced with every other
in a completely self-contained vision.

The color is high-spirited. A light blue dominates
from trimmings on cap, dress, and neckpiece; red-
blond hair, mauve drapery, pink lips, warm complex-
ion are kept soft and light to stay in key. The picture
is not altogether finished. Stuart worked only as long
as his vision held. We can see him sinking into a chair
after the girl left with the exhaustion of a mystic returned from reverie.

In *Augusta Montagu,* Stuart escaped from the conflict of his times the way Gainsborough often escaped,
into a world of the imagination where the personal vision of the dreamer rules. However, he was rarely able
to mount into that delectable world. Like Strephon,
he was supernatural only down to the waist. This is revealed by a curious dichotomy in many of his English
paintings. We have seen that late-nineteenth-century
critics were willing to believe that the landscape background in Stuart's *Gentleman Skating* was by the lyrical Gainsborough, but they preferred to attribute the
face to that downright portraitist Raeburn.

The stylistic contradictions which inspired such
judgments reflected a deep cleavage in Stuart's nature.

He was gay on the surface, sad below; superficially sure, but basically tortured and uncertain. The time was to come when, at least as far as his painting went, he was to build a bridge over this gap; the time was not yet. In many of his English and Irish portraits the backgrounds are painted with dash: trees and drapery and tresses are given a delightful movement and texture by a delicate stroking of the brush. His likenesses are quick and highspirited to the neck, and then suddenly grave and exact. He refused to stylize flesh as he stylized trees. He showed features with almost photographic accuracy; his pursuit of character was slow, deeply pondered, profound. For portraits in which he wished to excel, he urged the sitter to have a life mask made in plaster so that he could study more carefully the structure of the head.

That, despite their brilliance, his Gainsborough-esque backgrounds did not appeal profoundly to his nature is shown by one of the strangest facts in this strange man's career. His passport to success, *Gentleman Skating,* had shown a man in physical action before a well-defined landscape containing lesser figures; the setting and pose created a greater sensation than the subject's face. A painter of normal temperament would have followed up his triumph with other pictures in the same mode. But not Stuart. He had created the picture as a freak to attract attention. It had done so. That was enough. Critics of every generation who have discussed the canvas insist that Stuart could have been a great landscape-painter. He was not interested.

He was no more interested in conventionally elaborate portraits, but he undertook them sometimes under pressure from particular patrons. Thus he painted Lord St. Vincent, standing full-length on a bluff with a pygmy British fleet visible under his pointing arm. The picture is lost, but an engraving after it suggests that it was not very successful. Indeed, when Stuart had refused instruction in line drawing, he had deprived himself of the best means of composing a picture containing many sharply defined forms.

During 1784 the American millionaire William Bingham commissioned him to paint a conversation piece: it was to be an outdoor scene with trees, showing Bingham himself, a little girl in a wide hat, and Mrs. Bingham holding a baby on the back of a horse. Stuart purchased a suitably large canvas, and sketched in heads and shoulders, those of the adults brilliantly, those of the children well enough. Having added a few feet of the horse's back, he threw his brushes down and abandoned the project.

Whether or not Stuart ever completed a canvas containing more than two figures is not altogether clear; if he did, it would be a great prodigy in his style. Even double portraits that can be authoritatively attributed to his brush are scarce. He rarely painted a mother and child together; indeed, he avoided depicting children whenever he could. Among his more than one thousand pictures there are hardly a dozen likenesses of the very young.

With great perversity or single-mindedness—define it as you will—Stuart devoted his major energies to character studies of adult faces, and in his desire to probe deep he often offended the fashionably minded. He described to his friends how when a foppish doctor came for a first sitting, he surveyed the sartorial vision for a moment and then sat down to talk. The physician kept looking at his watch, and finally ventured: "Mr. Stuart, this is very entertaining, but you must be aware that my time is precious. I feel very uncomfortable."

"I am glad of it. I have felt so ever since you entered my studio."

"Why?"

"You look like a fool. Disarrange that fixed-up costume, and I will go to work." Stuart was concerned with people as God made them, not with the contributions of their tailors—or their perfumers.

When a lady appeared for a sitting well armed with rouge, he told her—for he was courtly to the ladies— that she was too lovely to seek exterior assistance. She should wash her face.

"Oh, Mr. Stuart, you have found me out?"

"Of course I have. Anyone having knowledge of

the human face knows there is a boundary to the color in every lady's cheek, and if you go beyond the line you will certainly be detected." He showed her the line. "But pray do not do it. You do not need it."

Stuart was considered particularly successful in painting professional men. When Alderman Boydell, the famous publisher of engravings, wished to preserve the features of London's leading artists in a gallery of portraits, he gave the commission to Stuart. Here was a task perfectly suited to the interests of the American; the fifteen pictures that resulted are amazingly various and profound. His likeness of Dominic Serres, the marine architect who was once a ship's master, shows us a mighty physique gone flabby with age and lack of exercise. The heavy body has become round-shouldered, and the once powerful face is now mild and fat, the mouth relaxed into a slightly foolish smile. Robert Thew, who rose from making barrels to making engravings, is a younger, more energetic man, an honest artisan turned part-time gentleman; he would bow low to a peer, but not hesitate to worst his lordship at a business deal.

Stuart's rendering of Sir Joshua Reynolds is cast in an elegiac mood. We see an aging social and artistic leader whose fine costume contrasts with his tired, half-cynical expression. Reynolds is sure of his position and jealous of his dignity, yet he seems to be looking down from his pinnacle of fame and pride and wondering a little, now that the end is near, what the long road and all the adulation signified. Sir Joshua is said to have disliked the portrait. But his first biographer, the anonymous author of *Testimony to the Genius of Sir Joshua Reynolds*, regarded it as the best of Reynolds's many likenesses.

Lack of professional success did not explain Stuart's sudden disappearance from the grand establishment on New Burlington Street. One day he was among the most admired artists in London; the next day no one knew where he and his family were. Newspapers described them variously as in America, where Stuart had gone to look after "a large tract of land, the property of his father"; or in Dublin; or in Paris. Even their best friends had no idea what had happened to them. So carefully did Stuart cover their trail that to this day we do not know where they spent the autumn of 1787. Undoubtedly their sudden departure was flight, flight from debts. "I knew Stuart well," Sir Thomas Lawrence said, "and I believe the real cause of his leaving England was his having become tired of the inside of some of our prisons." He owed eighty pounds for snuff alone.

CHAPTER SIX

IRISH VARIETIES

FINALLY, Stuart turned up with his family in Dublin. He had been invited there by the Duke of Rutland, recently appointed Lord Lieutenant of Ireland. Stuart was to state dramatically that on entering the city he met Rutland's funeral procession leaving it. His Grace was buried on November 17, 1787, a date that probably approximates the time of Stuart's arrival.

If rumor is correct, the painter had relied so heavily on the Duke's help that he had brought no money with him, and before he got round to making any, he was carried to debtor's prison. This was a spur to industry. He set up his easel behind the bars, and the local gentry flocked into prison to be painted by one of the most accomplished artists ever to visit their distant capital. Since it was Stuart's habit to charge half price at the first sitting—this practice, he insisted, had been urged on him by a delegation of his London admirers which included Rutland, Lord St. Vincent, and Colonel Barré—he soon had enough cash to pay off his debts, tip the jailer, and find a less unconventional spot in which to complete the portraits.

Debts amassed soon again. Whether or not at the time of his arrival, Stuart undoubtedly spent some time in a Dublin prison. His Irish crony, J. D. Herbert, gives an admiring account of his skill in recognizing bailiffs at several hundred yards, and his address at evading them. "So silly am I," Herbert quotes Stuart as saying, "and so careless of keeping out of debt, it has cost me more to bailiffs for my liberty than would pay the debts for which they would arrest me. I confess my folly in feeling proud of such feats."

A young painter, Herbert had met Stuart at a dinner given by a group of Dublin artists, where the American shared the role of guest of honor with another but less distinguished professional from London, Christopher Pack. Basking in the admiration of the provincials, Pack boasted that Sir Joshua Reynolds, when stumped by a particularly difficult piece of painting, made use of his help. Stuart downed a glass of wine and asked in a loud voice what was the speaker's name? On being told, he shouted: "Pack? Pack! Well, I've often heard of a pack of nonsense, but I never saw it before."

Having annihilated his fellow practitioner from the capital, Stuart delivered an oration of his own. He had started life, he confided, as a musician, and had gone to London to follow that art. The idea of painting had never occurred to him until he visited West's studio. When he asked to borrow a canvas and brushes, West laughed at the idea that a man with no training could paint, but Stuart sat right down and turned out a tolerable portrait. As Pack sat in vanquished silence, Stuart described West's amazed admiration.

Although Stuart loved to deflate the pompous, he was kind to beginners who came to him for help. He assisted the son of a Dublin linen-draper, George Place, to become a professional miniaturist. When John Comerford, a primitive painter from Kilkenny, visited Stuart, the results were so decisive that some thirty-five years later Comerford sent his former teacher this message: "He said that he owed more to you for what he is now (and he has an income of two thousand sterling and enjoying at the same time a considerable reputation as an artist) than to all the rest of the artists in the world besides."

The advice Stuart gave Martin Archer Shee had autobiographical overtones. Shee was nineteen, almost exactly the age at which Stuart had left Newport for London; he was a self-taught professional doing a brisk business in unsophisticated portraits; he doubted, as Stuart had done, the usefulness to his art of sophistication. Now expertly trained, Stuart urged Shee not to bury his talents in Dublin, where he could expect neither appreciation nor improvement. Obediently, Shee went to London, where he became a famous society portraitist, a knight, and President of the Royal Academy.

Older Irish painters found Stuart's arrival a catastrophe, for he monopolized the best business; even Robert Home, the leading native portraitist, was forced to flee to the provinces. The Irish equivalents of the toplofty aristocrats who had shied away from Stuart's studio in London flocked to him like crows to a cornfield. Stuart was not impressed by their birth, their airs, or their faces. It became very difficult to get him to finish a picture, "so fond was he of touching the half-price."

Herbert tells us that he "had all the equalizing spirit of the American, and looked contemptuously on titled rank." When Stuart depicted a daughter of the Arch-bishop of Dublin, he did not make the likeness flat-tering enough to suit her. Her complaints annoyed Stuart, and he simply stopped painting on the portrait. While Herbert was lounging in the studio several days later, a flunky announced that the Bishop was below in his carriage and wanted Stuart to come down and talk with him. Herbert rose to go.

"No," said Stuart. "You must stay and witness a novel scene." Then he sent down word that he was not used to attending on carriages, but that if the Bishop would come up to his painting-room he would speak to him. The servant returned in a minute to report that the Bishop's gout kept him from coming up. Stuart sent the flunky back with the message that he was extremely sorry for two reasons: one, for the

Bishop's sufferings; and two, that he had the rheuma-
tism himself. However, he would try to meet His
Grace halfway.

With a wink at Herbert he slipped off his shoe,
wrapped a silk handkerchief round his foot, and
limped exactly halfway down the stairs, where he
waited for the Bishop, who came limping painfully
up. "Well," Herbert heard the episcopal voice remark, "I have contrived to hobble up, you see, Mr.
Stuart. Sorry to see your foot tied up."

"Ha! Oh, dear!"

"Do you suffer very much with your foot?"

"Oh, very much, my lord."

The Bishop remonstrated that the picture of his
daughter was "not pleasing." With Stuart leading the
way, the two men limped slowly up the stairs to his
studio. Placing the picture on the easel, Stuart began
to lay a dark color on the background. The Bishop
watched him curiously, but when Stuart, continuing
the rhythmical sweep of his brush, laid color over the
face too, he remonstrated. "Now what are you doing? Are you painting it out?"

"Yes, I am putting Your Grace out of pain, as
much as I can. I shall return the half-price, and am
sorry I cannot please Your Grace."

The Bishop insisted he only wanted the face altered, not the whole picture destroyed. Stuart nodded
gravely, dipped some tow in turpentine, and removed

the color. Then he said: "A dressmaker may alter a dress, a milliner a cap, a tailor a coat, but a painter may give up his art if he attempts to alter to please. It cannot be done."

The Bishop bowed and hobbled away. Stuart attended him to the middle step of the stairs, bowed low, and returned jubilant with victory. He instructed his servant to take the picture to the Bishop's house, but not to leave it until he had collected fifteen guineas.

Obviously Stuart's rapid rise in the world had not made him a snob. The poverty of his young manhood had filled him with the desire to associate with the rich and fashionable, but when he reached this end, he was neither obsequious nor satisfied. Perhaps he realized that the Irish gentry, although they found his pranks and tall tales amusing, did not regard him as one of them. In any case, the American, having leaped the hurdle into high society, found it necessary to prove that society was not so high after all. He was like a young boxer who struggles to meet the world's champion, but only that he may knock him out. Herbert found that it was not Stuart's friendship with the rich but his "consciousness of his pre-eminence as a painter" that gave him the air of a coxcomb.

Stuart told a story which he may well have made up to show his opinion of ancestors. He said that an Irish merchant, who had got a castle by a fortunate speculation, sent for him to paint the portraits of his forebears. The painter assumed, of course, there would be drawings or miniatures to enlarge; on his arrival at the castle he found none. "How the deuce," he cried, "am I going to paint your ancestors if you have no ancestors?"

"Nothing easier. Go to work and paint such ancestors as I *ought* to have had."

Delighted, Stuart turned out a goodly company of knights in armor, judges with bushy wigs, and ladies depicted in the archaic manner with nosegays and lambs; ancestors which, he implied, did as well as the real article. A painter could be, if he cared so to demean himself, the equivalent of a college of heralds.

In Dublin, Stuart's reputation loomed so large that he was not forced to paint according to any taste except his own; his work became more fluent and more original than it had been in London. When induced to create an official portrait of conventional elegance, he did so in a spirit that seems close to parody.

Stuart's full-length of the noble earl who was Lord Chancellor of Ireland shows John Fitzgibbon's haughty yet sheeplike face almost swallowed up in its wig. The body is dwarfed by its robes of office, which are so encrusted with gold embroidery that they seem to be standing by themselves. Strewn round the picture are a gold mace with a gold crown on top; the chancellor's purse, embroidered with the arms of Britain and most mightily tasseled; an overfed stone column; an old rose curtain dangling from nowhere; and, of course, a brightly tinted sunset sky. How Stuart must have laughed up his sleeve as he listened to the breathless eulogies of the local esthetes!

Most of the portraits Stuart painted in Ireland are very simply composed: the likeness of the future admiral, the Honorable Thomas Pakenham, is typical. First we are struck, as Stuart wanted us to be, by the face: one of those Anglo-Saxon countenances that are quite vacant on the surface. A French adversary might have mistaken the sea-dog for a dolt whose intelligence was suited only to converse with foxhounds. But the Frenchman, and this Stuart indicates most deftly, would have been courting trouble. Behind the sleepy eyes, the blank forehead, the receding chin, a practical and intolerant mind moves with all the force of an excellent instrument which has been swept clean, by birth and by training, of wonder and self-doubt.

The subtlety of this character study is more than matched by the subtlety of the colors. The head is silhouetted against an abstraction of a sunset sky: mottled red shading off to patches of grayish blue. Echoing and contrasting are two other reds, a creamy pink collar and the delicate pink-to-carmine mottling of the face. A mauve-green medal, chiming with the gray hair, brings in another range of tints, but basically this picture is a brilliant exercise in reds.

Stuart lived for a while in the city, on Pill Lane, but soon bought a farm at Stillorgan. The exact size of the family he took with him to this fashionable suburb it is impossible to know, for records concerning Stuarts other than the resplendent husband and father are startlingly meager. The best evidence indicates that during his lifetime Gilbert had twelve children, ten girls and two boys, but specific information can be found concerning only the one boy and four girls who lived to maturity. Even about these there is much confusion. Thus, one of the younger daughters assumed that the son who survived, Charles Gilbert Stuart, was "my second brother," although it would seem that he was the oldest child, since he was born hardly a year after his parents were married. The burial records of the girls contain an impossible figure: Agnes is said to have died in 1850 at the age of seventy, which would mean that she was born when her mother was twelve years old. She may well have been the second child Dunlap tells us appeared in London. Emma, if her tombstone is worthy of credence, was born in Ireland, late in 1790 or early in 1791. Jane was many years younger. What other babies came, lived briefly, and died remains a total mystery.

As an older woman, Mrs. Stuart was usually loath to talk of the Irish years: "It gave my mother pain,"

Jane noted, "to remember anything associated with
reckless extravagance, or what she called his folly."
When in a rarely communicative mood, she would
say that her husband "was delighted with the society
he met in Ireland. The elegant manners, the wit, and
the hospitality of the upper-class Irish suited his genial
temperament. . . . The gentlemen of the surround-
ing neighborhood constituted his principal society."
Such statements glossed over Stuart's democratic and
bohemian tendencies—Herbert says that he made a
point of not dining at a rich house if asked to a poor
one—but on other matters Mrs. Stuart was frank:

"I am sorry to say that Stuart entered too much into
their [his friends'] convivialities. The fact is that it was
his misfortune, I might say his curse . . . to have
been sought after by society. . . . The consequence
was that he gave dinner parties as was the fashion of
the day. . . .

"After one of these dinner parties, composed of
some of the wits of the day, among them the Rev. Mr.
Best, Dean Beatson, and John Kemble, a violent dispute arose as to the possession of the truest eye. It was
finally proposed that there should be a mark placed
in the garden that the question might be decided by
pistols." Stuart's reputation, it seems, enabled him to
get away with even the oldest joke, for, after several
shots had been fired, he convulsed the company by
standing in front of the target as the safest place.

Between parties and portrait sittings, Stuart tried to find surcease for his tortured nerves in tending his little farm. Planting the rich soil, watching the un-hurried growth of flowers, he forgot for a little while the dissatisfaction of his spirit. There in the rural land-scape, the world of fame and fashion seemed as unim-portant as a dream. He could relax a little.

When Herbert visited Stillorgan, he found Stuart before the house, tending some flowerpots. "He then took me to his garden, which was well-cropped, all by his own hands, walked me over the grounds, and pointed out his skill in farming. . . . I cordially confessed that I should rather see his works in his painting-room, that I was ignorant of farming, garden-ing, or feeding pigs. He pitied me very much, observ-ing what a loss I sustained by not attending to the cul-tivation of that on which mankind were supported and rendered wealthy and powerful." Herbert found that the artist was more pleased by praise of his "very pretty pigs" than by "anything I could say in praise of his pictures."

When Stuart's ever mounting debts made it seem expedient to flee from Ireland, he played one last trick on the gentlemen who had been his companions and patrons. He began many pictures which he had no intention of completing, demanding the usual half-payment at each first sitting. "The artists of Dublin," he told Herbert, "will get employment in finishing them. You may reckon on making something handsome by it, and I shan't regret my default when a friend is benefited by it in the end. The possessors will be well off. The likeness is there, and the finishing may be better than I should have made it."

Stuart had promised to go to London, where several commissions awaited him, but at the last moment he changed his mind; perhaps he discovered his creditors were awaiting him too. He set sail with his family to New York.

CHAPTER SEVEN

THE RETURN OF THE PRODIGAL

AT the moment of his leaving Ireland, Stuart stepped into the realm of legend, for he had started on the journey that was to end with the most famous pictures in American history, his portraits of Washington. Stuart's *Washingtons* haunt us all from the cradle to the grave; they stare at us from primers and posters and postage stamps; indeed, it is these canvases, not the hand of God, which determined how the father of their country would look to most future Americans. It has often been pointed out that, should Washington return to earth today, he would be regarded as an impostor if he did not look like Stuart's portraits.

Since the figure of Washington—the cherry-tree Washington—which is pounded into every schoolboy's brain is as mythological as Prometheus, it is natural that a full-blown mythology should surround the hero's most famous likenesses. It is authoritatively reported, for instance, that Stuart nobly gave up a brilliant European future because of a patriotic desire to preserve the features of the man in the world he most admired. We know that Stuart was driven from the British Isles by debt. Stories he himself told do not reveal deep admiration for Washington; he appears to have been incapable of venerating any man, even his beloved benefactor West.

It is true, however, that the idea of painting Washington was partly responsible for Stuart's return to America. Harassed by debt, casting around for a new source of income, he remembered that the President was one of the most popular men in the world. "I expect to make a fortune by Washington alone," he told Herbert. "I calculate upon making a plurality of portraits, whole-lengths that will enable me to realize; and if I should be fortunate, I will repay my English and Irish creditors." Upon several other occasions he spoke of the large sums he hoped to make from an engraving after a popular portrait of the Father of his Country.

The Stuart family were accompanied on their trip to America by a miniaturist, Walter Robertson. This son of a Dublin jeweler was to do a brisk business copying life-size Stuart portraits onto small chips of ivory that could be carried, like a modern snapshot, in locket or pocket. The two men got bored on the boat, drank too much, and once, after he had been insulted by Stuart, Robertson reeled to his stateroom for pistols, and returned demanding a duel. The captain separated the painters, who, on the following morning, resumed their friendship.

When he reached New York late in 1792 or early in 1793, Stuart rented a house in the fashionable section, on Stone Street, large enough to hold both his family and a painting-room. The method he had used in England to attract patrons, hanging his own show in a private gallery, was unavailable to him, since every portrait he had painted in England and Ireland had been sold; he had brought home with him no samples of his style. However, his reputation had traveled before him, in particular to two Irish-American merchants, George and Hugh Pollack, whose sister Stuart had painted in Dublin. They may well have lent him money; they certainly ordered their portraits. When George visited Philadelphia in November 1794, Stuart gave him a letter to Joseph Anthony saying that he owed more to the Pollacks "than the world beside." His hope that his relations would find his patron agreeable was more than accomplished, for within six months George Pollack was married to Stuart's cousin Martha Anthony.

After a few of the blank canvases Stuart had undoubtedly brought with him, since artists' supplies were not manufactured in the United States, blossomed into likenesses of New Yorkers, he was besieged with commissions, for he was the strongest painter to practice in America since Copley's departure in 1774, the most sophisticated these shores had ever known. Even Dunlap, who had studied abroad with West, felt that he had "never seen portraits before, so decidedly was form and mind conveyed." Stuart's talents, Dunlap continued, "introduced him to the intimate society of all who were distinguished by office, rank, or attainment." The London diarist Farington recorded gossip that "his prices were not so great as he had in England," but added: "His expenses are proportionally more reasonable."

Eighteen years before, Stuart had left America as an obscure youth whose cocksureness hid doubt; now he returned a famous man, but little changed in character. He felt a tremendous need to make a mighty impression. There were unpleasant memories to exorcise, both personal and artistic. We can only guess at the troubles of his childhood from the scars left on his character; those scars were deep. Certain it is that although Stuart lived near to Rhode Island for twenty-three years, he returned to the scenes of his youth only once, and then when he was a very old man.

Determining to dazzle New York, Stuart temporarily shelved his dislike of elaborate pictures. His portraits of Don and Doña Josef de Jaudenes y Nebot, a Spanish consul and his wife, were among his most serious attempts to work in the aristocratic tradition. Virtuosity leaps from each square inch of canvas. A jewel is brilliantly indicated with two brush-sweeps of contrasting colors; the highlight on the head of the Don's cane is a luscious streak of yellow pigment; the draperies are painted crisply and surely, the textures indicated with brilliant economy of means. And the

faces, although prettied up as is suitable in such portraits, are not completely vapid. The woman is more
than a doll, and the man even shows a little force.
Why then are the pictures not more impressive?

Stuart himself could have given the answer; he
must have felt it in the very hand that placed the pigment on the canvas. He was not interested in what he
was doing. This was an exercise, played brilliantly
but by rote. After he had finished the pictures, he may
well have shaken his wild head angrily and sworn:
"Never again." To this we can only say: "Amen."

On the other extreme is Stuart's *Petrus Stuyvesant*.
Rarely has a disagreeable personality been recorded
more truthfully. The face of the New York Crœsus
and patrician is an unhealthy, bilious red; his tiny, wa-
tery blue eyes squint nearsightedly, and the depression
on the bridge of his nose left by his eyeglasses is
clearly indicated. His mouth is drawn back in an expression of weak irritability. Perversely, as if to show
that the clothes are finer than the man, Stuart has
painted Stuyvesant's golden-hued waistcoat with startling brilliance. A few quick strokes with a heavily
loaded brush reveal the crumpled but expensive cloth.

Stuart was so much the social rage that he could get
away with anything. Gravely and proudly, Stuyvesant carried his "Stuart" home.

During his New York period, Stuart painted General Horatio Gates. Son of a duke's housekeeper in

England, Gates had entered the British army and had managed, by a mixture of servility and energy, to rise to a surprising rank for one of his low birth; he became a major. At last the tightrope he had to walk with his social superiors—who also became his military superiors with the speed of light—disgusted Gates. He retired onto a Virginia plantation. When his personal revolt against the British caste system swept him into the American Revolutionary army, he became not a major but a major general. He commanded at the only great victory achieved by unaided American arms: the Battle of Saratoga. Congress was impressed into thinking him an abler soldier than Washington, and Washington accused Gates of scheming to overthrow him, a charge which still divides historians into bickering camps. Eventually Gates was entrusted with the southern army. Now the goddess of war turned on her former favorite; his troops suffered at Camden one of the worst defeats of the Revolution. Congress liked victors, but not losers; his military career was brought to an end amid charges of inefficiency, cowardice. In retirement and disgrace, the old soldier was wandering disconsolately through the fields of his Virginia plantation when a sound of martial music filled the air and Washington's army marched by to support the French fleet in the crowning triumph of Yorktown.

After the war, Gates's reputation gradually

mended; he became a social leader; he married an
heiress. But the housekeeper's son was never quite
easy as he sat with patricians in warmth and splendor
and luxury. He would steal away from elegant company to help inconspicuous devils who had served in
his armies; his wife's money flowed from his purse
into ragged pockets. Even such liberal alms could not
quiet his conscience for long. Over the salvers full of
sweetmeats in his dining-room black faces showed ac-
cusingly. He freed his slaves and moved to New
York, where he came under the brush of Stuart.

Various conventional roads lay open to the painter.
The most obvious would have been to show Gates as
a warrior exulting over victories past. Or Stuart could
have shown the slippery character who had—or so
they said—schemed against Washington. Stuart could
have exalted the democrat, or attacked the radical. He
did none of these things, and he did all of them.

Before us is an image as humanly complicated as a
modern biography. Our first glance tells us that Gates
was not happy, and that he was tired. The world and
all its trappings are here displayed: a fine uniform;
epaulettes; two medals, one as large as a saucer; a cere-
monial sword. Yet all this pomp seems to mean nothing to the old, unhealthy face that shows above it.
The shoulders sag as if under the weight of the epaulettes, and the hand on the sword leans like the hand
of an invalid on his cane. The face and the huge

medal are the two centers of attention in the picture: each seems a sad commentary on the other.

The more we look at the face, the more concerned we become. There are good things here, and terrible things. Those eyes have seen angels and devils, and sometimes the two have waltzed together. The expression about the mouth might be ill-humor; or is it discouragement, or fear? The skin of the cheeks is relaxed, as if the warrior no longer had the energy to keep his features active.

The sense of disillusionment, of the vanity of worldly things, of a longing for death, which the picture conveys is heightened by its stylistic resemblance to conventional pictures expressing emotions exactly opposite. By making only the most subtle changes, a copyist could transform this canvas into a standard likeness of a conquering hero. Smooth out the face a little, straighten the back, add some bayonets and smoke to the background, and—presto!—it would be done. Yet Stuart's picture is far from being a parody. It is a new vision based on tragic emotions as deep in the artist as in the sitter.

Stuart has subdued all the colors to the red of the face, which is echoed by a blob of red in the sky to the lower left. The General stands before an open-air scene in which all aspects of landscape have been reduced to hints. A brown billowing at his back indicates trees. To the left, the line where earth meets sky is clear, but all else is generalized to indications of light. We see bands of orange-yellow and blue; uneven masses of muffled red and brown: these give an impression of earth and water which is less representational than emotional. The painters of the future were to evolve theories on what Stuart did by instinct.

During the summer of 1774 Stuart undertook a portrait of John Jay which he wished to be especially impressive, since he hoped to have the likeness of the popular Federalist leader engraved. He was interrupted by what he called "a smart attack of fever and ague," and when he returned to his easel, nothing came out right. "Would you believe," Mrs. Jay wrote her husband on August 2, "that Stuart has not yet sent me your picture? . . . He has at length resumed the pencil, and your nephew has been sitting with your robe for him."

Although Mrs. Jay considered the likeness her husband's "very self," Stuart remained unsatisfied. Under ordinary circumstances he would have kept the importunate wife waiting, but he did need permission to make and sell the engraving. "Just as I put my pen aside to take tea," Mrs. Jay continued, "Mr. Stuart arrived with your picture. He insisted on my promising it would be destroyed when he presented me with a better one, which he said he certainly would if you would be so obliging as to have a [life] mask made for him. In ten days he goes to Philadelphia to take a likeness of the President."

Ever since his return to America almost two years before, Stuart had put off painting the portrait, from which he hoped to make his fortune, of the international hero who was so much greater than he; he continued to procrastinate. Philadelphia, where Washington was presiding over the federal government, did not see him in the ten days Mrs. Jay had mentioned. After a month, Stuart wrote Joseph Anthony that he hoped to be at the capital in three weeks. "The object of my journey is only to secure a picture of the President, and finish yours. My other engagements [in New York] are such as totally preclude the possibility of my encouraging the most distant idea that any other application can have effect at present."

Stuart never journeyed to Philadelphia for the specific purpose of painting Washington. He stayed in New York until he had skimmed the cream off that portrait market. Then, early in 1795, he moved with his family and all his possessions to the fresher pastures of the national capital.

He found there the most aristocratic society ever connected with American politics. The well-born leaders of the Federalist Party, who had regarded the Revolution as a quarrel between the British and American upper classes for control over the American people, were now in power. While Hamilton organized the country's financial structure to nurture that propertied minority which he considered the necessary backbone of all stable governments, the provincial aristocrats tried to establish an imitation of the British Court, where they could play the parts of lords and ladies. What if the poor devils who had starved at Valley Forge wondered if they had suffered for this: the salons of Philadelphia were full of beautiful ladies who thought monarchy divine.

For the gay society of the capital was dominated by rich and beautiful women. How graciously they bowed to Federalist politicians, who bowed as graciously back! If you looked through half-closed eyes, you might imagine you were in London or Versailles. The opposition leaders who agreed with Jefferson that the masses should be given a voice in government were rarely invited to such parties; and when they were, the ladies were delighted to conclude that they did not know how to behave.

The most brilliant salon of this period, probably the most brilliant ever held in the United States, was presided over by Hamilton's ally and Stuart's patron from his London years, Mrs. William Bingham, the wife of the war profiteer and merchant speculator who was considered America's richest citizen. The beauty of this "uncrowned queen of the Federalist group" is attested to by Stuart's portraits of her. Her drawing-room was decorated entirely with furniture imported from abroad, as was only proper. To the pleasure of the other provincial belles, she introduced the foreign custom of having a long line of footmen announce arriving guests. When democrats had to be asked for political reasons, this sometimes led to misunderstandings. There was, for instance, the sad experience of James Monroe; had it been suggested that he might someday be President, every beautiful feminine shoulder shining bare under Mrs. Bingham's chandeliers would have risen in horror.

"Senator Monroe!" announced a flunky.

The Senator looked up good-humoredly. "Coming."

"Senator Monroe!" echoed another flunky down the hall.

"Coming as soon as I can get my greatcoat off."

One was forced to put up with such unfortunate happenings for the time being, until the government of the United States was put on a sound aristocratic basis, but after that you would not even have to half close your eyes to believe that Philadelphia was London.

Having taken a house on the southeast corner of Sixth and Chestnut streets, Stuart enjoyed to the full the pleasures of the capital. Loving, as his family complained, "the pleasures of the table to excess," he feasted in mansions, and was enchanted to see his own

guests enjoy fine food and expensive wine which he
bankrupted himself to serve. That Mrs. Stuart was
present when he entertained at home it is impossible
to doubt, although she made no recorded impression
on the revelers. Probably she sat thinking of bills for
necessities that remained unpaid, silent in her disap-
proval of what she called "his folly."

Memoirs dilate on her husband's hilarious stories,
his musical skill, his wit and courtliness. When the
beautiful Mrs. Perez Morton, locally known as "the
American Sappho," wrote a poem on the portrait of
her he had painted, Stuart replied with a poem of his
own that put Sappho's in the shade:

> Who would not glory in the wreath of praise
> Which M—— offers in her polished lays?
> I feel their cheerful influence at my heart,
> And more complacent I review my art.
> Yet, ah, with Poesy, that gift divine,
> Compar'd, how poor, how impotent is mine!
> What though my pencil trace the hero's form,
> Trace the soft female cheek with beauty warm:
> No further goes my power; 'tis thine to spread
> Glory's proud ensign o'er the hero's head;
> 'Tis thine to give the chief a deathless name,
> And tell to ages yet unborn his fame;
> 'Tis thine to future period to convey
> Beauty enshrined in some immortal lay.

No faithful portrait now Achilles shows,
With Helen's matchless charms no canvas glows;
But still in mighty Homer's verse portrayed,
N'er can her beauty or his glory fade.
No wonder if in tracing charms like thine,
Thought and expression blend in rich design;
'Twas heaven itself that blended in thy face
The lines of reason with the lines of grace.
'Twas heaven that bade the swift idea rise,
Paint thy soft cheek and sparkle in thine eyes:
Invention there could justly claim no part,
I only boast the copyist's humble art. . . .

The gaiety of his environment inspired Stuart to execute a series of portraits that lifts him to a high place among depictors of beautiful women. But even in such pictures he saw the human animal beneath the social, the sexual mask. Lovely ladies, as they sometimes discover to their sorrow, are in the minds of the world an abstraction, a dream of grace and gentleness and charm. Stuart was not much of a dreamer.

The best of his portraits of the American Sappho was found unfinished in his studio after his death. Perhaps he was caught with the beauty of the picture as it stood and resolved to keep this evidence of inspiration; perhaps the sitter found the likeness too shrewd. The visible brushstrokes show with what excitement Stuart had painted. But the poetess is hardly a classic muse; we see a social warrior, heroine of a thousand skirmishes in drawing-room and boudoir. At the age of a little more than forty, she is a fading belle, holding off the years with the wits and arts of an able woman. The wisdom of experience and the coldness of a sharp and calculating mind have covered the fires that may once have flushed her cheeks with blushes— but only to bank more violent heat within. Although Stuart noticed that her figure was beginning to go, he gave her face the fine, thin temper of a rapier.

How Mrs. Morton must have despised that "fine, portly, buxom dame"—the daughter of a boarding-house-keeper—who with the tragic downfall of the aristocrats and the election of that dangerous Jacobin, Jefferson, was to step into Mrs. Bingham's shoes as the social queen of the national capital. From Stuart's portrait, Dolly Madison, the Quaker lass who had just married her Senator, looks at us with grave, vulnerable eyes. If the American Sappho was a tiger, Mrs. Madison was a hearth-bred kitten who suspected that you got further in the world with purrs than with slashes of spikelike talons. She made friends by listening quietly, and agreeing with soft sympathy; she seemed actually to admire boors like Senator Monroe. This was the woman who was to be amused rather than ashamed when the British ambassador said her official dinners resembled "harvest home suppers." Mrs. Morton or Mrs. Bingham would have *died!*

Although her soft and piquant face is a little too heavy for modern styles, Ann Penn Allen, daughter of the founder of Allentown, Pennsylvania, was considered "one of the most splendid beauties this country ever produced." Stuart built her portrait around the light blue of her eyes. That color is echoed in the scarf below her breasts, and re-echoed, with increasing delicacy, in the ribbon that binds her hair, in a touch on the shoulder, in the lacy band about her neck, in a muffled squiggle in the lower-right background. Looking closely, we see there are bits of blue everywhere: in the whites of the eyes, in the mottling of the flesh.

When composing the background, Stuart amused himself with a cliché which had been repeated by generations of polite portraitists. To break their compositions with an interesting vertical line, and to allow a play between shallow space behind the head and deep space elsewhere, painters from Van Dyck on had inserted their sitters before cliffs which, two thirds of the way across the picture, dropped off sharply, their edges gracefully festooned with trailing vines or leaves. In Stuart's picture, a flat but variegated dark brown ceases suddenly in a falling line. The edge is coated with an irregular green ribbon which toward the top becomes darker and then gives way to round forms of green and black, touched here and there with orange. Beyond these shapes, Stuart picks up again his dominant blue note, lightening it in the center with

a pink flush. We have to be familiar with the iconog-
raphy of European art to recognize cliff, foliage, sunset sky. Stuart has stylized an old device into an almost
abstract element of color and design.

All through his American career, Stuart was caught
upon occasion with the splendor of a woman. Usually
these flashes of fire were kindled by creatures who had
more than the agreeable coloring and soft harmonious-
ness of youth; he admired a strong nose, firm eyes,
and a mouth pulled a little tight by knowledge of the
world. Sometimes pretty young things actuated not his
admiration but his sense of humor. Never did a
middle-aged man paint a more amused likeness of a
brash and chirpy belle than Stuart's *Mrs. Philip Jeremiah Schuyler*, executed about 1807.

Mrs. Schuyler's husband was real quality: out of a
Van Rensselaer by the mighty General Philip Schuyler. She herself came from a prominent family in
Newburyport. All this bored Stuart. He regarded the
twenty-one-year-old social force as a pert nincompoop
who, by being active and cute and outrageous and important all at once, had succeeded in having herself
considered beautiful and intelligent and witty. We can
see her flitting through a drawing-room, being gracious
one moment, grave the next, sitting down at the harpsichord to sing a tune with more spirit than melody,
always eliciting praise because she was so sure she de-
served it. Stuart accentuated the receding chin under

her full lips, the long nose; he mocked the elaborate ringlets. Yet he made her social triumphs believable too. Though shallow, the face on the canvas is bright; it has nice brown eyes and great vivacity.

As is often the case in Stuart's female portraits, the picture is given more than half its charm by the beauty of its color: a blue scarf with lighter-blue highlights falling off the near shoulder and wrapped around the far arm; a pink-and-cream face; a pearly white dress, all showing up brilliantly before a background that shades from black to luminous gray. He liked to paint women in blue.

Stuart had no interest in immaturity. Buds did not whisper to him of innocence and springtime, nor was he moved by the unrealized promise of an unopened flower. Above all, he hated things and creatures that were cute. He classed children and animals together, almost always refusing to paint either. But it was impossible to drive from his studio marriageable young girls such as Isabella Henderson Lenox, whose body was mature but whose mind had no substance that Stuart could catch. He did not, as Romney would have done, draw a lyrical vision seen through the eyes of an adolescent lover. He used his skill in reproducing the appearance of reality to put down the bright surface coloring and the agreeable texture of the young woman's face. He gave her an alive expression; we can see that she was pretty enough to draw young

men like flies to honey. Yet the interior emptiness of
the image evokes a strange sensation. This creature
looks human, yet we have our doubts. She is a mind-
less automaton, fashioned from hair and eyes and skin.

Old ladies had often inspired Stuart's American
predecessors to their happiest efforts. Copley, for instance, painted them with brilliant insight. Perhaps
unconsciously, he realized that the women of his time,
although often stronger-minded than their males, were
forced during most of their lives to hold their intellects
in check. First they were curtsying little girls; then
gentle young ladies blushing at the supposedly un-
expected attention given them by men; then responsible housewives and mothers who might not damage
family prestige by any frowardness. Only in their last
years did women escape from their shackles. Grand-
mothers now, dressed with illusive demureness in lace
caps, they pounded on the floor with their canes and
made their males stutter before them as they reported
with hardheaded cynicism the things that had been
stored up in the back of the brain by those soft brown
eyes that it was assumed had noticed nothing. Copley
appreciated this release, gloried in it, and lovingly put
the outrageous old beldames on canvas.

Stuart, however, loved the prime of life; to him,
old age was most admirable when it continued the pat-
terns of the middle years. Under his brush, grand-
mothers became faded belles; he admired the courage

that enabled them to continue after what he considered the best parts of their lives were over. He saw not autumnal glory, but the sadness of approaching winter.

Shortly after his return to America, he painted an aging matron in the Copley manner, perhaps inspired by one of his predecessor's pictures that he saw hanging on a local wall. The subject was Mrs. Richard Yates, wife of a partner of the Pollocks. Instead of urging her to defy the years, he dwelt on her old-lady's cap and showed her at her sewing. The conception is the conception of Copley, but the result could hardly be more different. The color, a harmony of pearly gray and white, is much more suave than anything the home-grown Colonial achieved, and Mrs. Yates herself is no delighted harridan romping through her second childhood. As the modern critic Gordon Washburn has pointed out, this is not Little Red Riding Hood's grandmother; we see rather the shrewd, rapacious face of the wolf who ate Grandmother and, for well-calculated purposes of his own, put on her clothes.

Since in those years men were encouraged to grow in more diverse ways than ladies, the male faces Stuart painted were more various than the female ones. His best pictures are likely to be those of men, and also his worst. When a merchant or dandy bored him, he could not, as he did with dull girls, fall back on ring-

lets of hair and frilly costumes. He turned out pictures
that are as uninteresting to the viewer as they were
to him.

But when he was really interested in a male face,
he painted with that compound of insight, sympathy,
and scientific detachment which is the ideal of modern
biographers. Himself one of the most tortured and ir-
rational of men, he realized that the basic motivation
of angry people is not anger, of avaricious people is
not greed. The very fact that his portraits are so profound might make them seem to the casual viewer
uncommunicative. Study, however, will bring out the
depth of Stuart's insight.

William Ellery Channing, the Unitarian divine
who went halfway toward Transcendentalism and
then stopped, the orator whose sermons led both to
abolition and civil war, is shown as a bodyless intel-
lectual with tousled hair, from whose small face little
blue eyes stare with a boldness that covers timidity.
John Quincy Adams, son of a president and soon to
be one himself, is a fat-faced, balding man, able but
uninspired, with a smile both cynical and soft. His
presidential predecessor, James Monroe, has a tired
face, far from beauty: thick nose, small eyes, flabby
chin. There is reluctant wisdom in the features, as if
Monroe had looked deeper into the human spirit than
it was wise to look, but had accepted his findings with
tolerance slightly tinged with sadness.

On the other side of the historian's conventional hierarchies Stuart depicted the arch-villain of text-books, Aaron Burr; writers have criticized the painting for omitting horns and a tail. It shows a young man, too handsome and charming for his own good, whose level gray eyes reveal not cynicism, but a grave, questioning naïveté. Perhaps in this canvas lies hidden the key to the Burr mystery. Were that swashbuckling trip down the Mississippi, that heated conference on Blennerhassett's Island, not after all the treason of a calculating schemer, but rather the toy of a child, a child who has not yet discovered the line between reason and fantasy?

Although Stuart objected to elaboration of costume, he never painted people in dishabille; nor did he substitute for the grandiloquent gestures he expunged the relaxations of private behavior. An eighteenth-century man of the world, he was bored by women in their role as mothers: whether or not a man went home to his family seemed to him an unimportant idiosyncrasy. He never bothered to paint his own wife or any of his own children. Stuart lighted personalities with the glare of Mrs. Bingham's chandeliers and caught the images they threw in the great mirrors of society.

CHAPTER EIGHT

IMAGES OF WASHINGTON

SHORTLY after his arrival in Philadelphia, Stuart had left his card and a letter of introduction from John Jay at Washington's house. He departed for a visit to the country, and, on his return a few days later, found awaiting him an invitation, signed by the President's secretary, for that very evening.

Ushered unceremoniously into a large chamber filled with company, Stuart assumed that he was in an anteroom where he was to wait with his fellow guests for admission into the presence of the most famous man in the world. No one seemed to notice him until a tall figure separated from a group in a distant corner, walked over, and addressed him by name. Recognizing Washington, Stuart was, for once, flustered. With affable condescension both helpful and irritating to a pathologically proud nature, Washington kept up an easy conversation until Stuart had recovered his composure. He then introduced the painter to the statesmen and aristocrats with whom he was surrounded.

Before Stuart departed, he secured the President's promise to sit; it was reluctantly given. Washington had been besieged by painters for years, and even during the making of his first portrait he had rebelled at the drudgery. "Inclination having yielded to importunity," he had moaned in 1772, "I am now, contrary to all expectation, under the hands of Mr. [C. W.] Peale, but in so grave, so sullen a mood, and now and then under the influence of Morpheus when some critical strokes are making, that I fancy the skill of this gentleman's pencil will be put to it in describing to the world what manner of man I am."

As Washington's fame increased, so did the demands of the painters. In 1785, when he was submitting to the efforts of the English artist Robert Edge Pine, Washington wrote: "In for a penny, in for a pound is an old adage. I am so hackneyed to the touches of the painter's pencil that I am now altogether at their beck, and sit like Patience on a monument, whilst they are delineating the lines of my face. It is a proof, among many other, of what habit and custom can effect. At first I was as impatient at the request, and as restive under the operation, as a colt is of the saddle. The next time I submitted very reluctantly, but with less flouncing; now, no dray moves more readily to the thrill than I do to the painter's chair."

When Stuart undertook his long-delayed Washington portrait in September 1795, he had no interest in depicting "patience on a monument." A skilled conversationalist, he relied on keeping the faces of his sitters animated by talking to them about their interests. "To military men," Waterhouse tells us, "he spoke of battles by sea and land; with the statesman on Hume's and Gibbon's histories; with the lawyer on jurisprudence or remarkable criminal trials; with the merchant in his way; with the man of leisure in his way; with the ladies in all ways. When putting the rich farmer on the canvas, he would go along with him from seed to harvest time; he would descant on the nice points of horse, ox, cow, sheep, or pig, and surprise him with his just remarks in the progress of making cheese and butter, or astonish him with his profound knowledge of manures. . . . He had wit at will, always ample, sometimes redundant."

Stuart discovered that all his powers would be needed to bring his sitter's face alive. He complained that the instant Washington started to sit, "an apathy seemed to seize him, and a vacuity spread over his countenance most appalling to paint." Having ruefully surveyed the iron countenance before him, Stuart ventured to remark: "Now, sir, you must let me forget that you are General Washington and that I am Stuart the painter."

"Mr. Stuart," Washington replied politely, "need never feel the need of forgetting who he is, or who General Washington is." His face was stony as ever.

Stuart grasped his brush harder and changed his attack; he resolved "to awaken the heroic spirit in him by talking of battles." The General looked up in surprise for a moment and then sank back into his boredom, for he had no intention of discussing military tactics with an artist. Rebuffed again, Stuart painted in silence for a while, but he could hardly bear to look at his canvas; the face that was rising before him was dead, though firm and powerful; he felt he had not got even a glimpse of Washington's real character. With the energy of despair, he set his facile tongue moving on the republican days of antiquity; like an angler using different flies on a wary trout, he dangled Cincinnatus in front of Washington, and Brutus, and the noble Cato. But to no avail.

Thus the sittings passed. On only one recorded occasion did the painter strike a spark from the General. As Stuart was allowing his tongue to idle on, no longer in hopes of rousing his sitter, but merely to keep the silence down, he launched on an old and hoary joke. He told the President how James II, on a journey through England to gain popularity, arrived in a town where the Mayor, who was a baker, was so frightened that he forgot his speech of welcome and stood there stammering. A friend jogged the Mayor's elbow and whispered: "Hold up your head and look like a man." When Stuart told how the flustered baker had repeated this admonition to the King, Washington's stern face unbelievably broke into a smile. But before Stuart could lift his brush, the smile was gone.

According to that rival painter Trumbull, "Mr. Stuart's conversation could not interest Washington;

he had no topic fitted for his character; the President did not relish his manners. When he sat to me, he was at his ease." This statement, influenced though it was by jealousy, probably contained some truth, since Stuart's exaggerated talk and showy erudition may well have displeased the old, tired statesman, among whose great virtues were love of truth and dislike for vain show.

Stuart could not keep from making jokes about the hero, even to the hero's wife. While he was painting Washington, Charles Willson Peale, the doting patriarch of a large family of painters, also secured a promise of sittings. He laid a trap for the President. Once Washington was well seated before his easel, the door opened noiselessly. James, Rembrandt, and Raphaelle Peale tiptoed in one by one and put up their easels. "I looked in to see how the old gentleman was getting on with the picture," Stuart later told his pupil John Neagle, "and to my astonishment I found the General surrounded by the whole family. They were peeling him, sir. As I went away, I met Mrs. Washington. 'Madam,' said I, 'the General's in a perilous situation.'

" 'How, sir?'

" 'He is beset, madam. No less than five upon him at once. One aims at his eye; another at his nose; another is busy with his hair; his mouth is attacked by the fourth; and the fifth has him by the button. In short, madam, there are five painters at him, and you who know how much he suffered when only attended by one, can judge of the horrors of his situation.' "

Such banter must have displeased the patrician lady, who, when she found a grease spot on the wall behind a chair, accused her niece of entertaining "a filthy democrat."

When Stuart's portrait of Washington was shown in Philadelphia, it was highly praised, although Stuart himself felt it a failure. We can get some idea of the effect he had wished to achieve from the word picture he gave of the President: "There were features in his face totally different from what I had observed in any other human being. The sockets of the eyes, for instance, were larger than what I ever met with before, and the upper part of the nose broader. All his features were indicative of the strongest passions; yet like Socrates his judgment and self-command made him appear a man of different cast in the eyes of the world."

Despite his dissatisfaction with his picture, Stuart took advantage of the financial opportunities it offered. Keeping possession of the original, so that no one else could make and sell copies, he himself made some fifteen copies which he sold for substantial sums. These canvases, which show the right side of Washington's face, are known as examples of the Vaughan type, since the first to be engraved was that taken to Eng-

land by Samuel Vaughan, an American merchant
resident in London, and reproduced as an illustration
in Lavater's *Essays in Physiognomy*.

While turning out his Vaughan portraits, Stuart
agitated for another chance to paint the President. In
April 1796 his opportunity came through Mr. and
Mrs. William Bingham, who persuaded Washington
to stand for a full-length they wished to give the famous British Whig, Lord Lansdowne. "It is notorious," writes Washington's adopted son, G. W. P.
Custis, "that it was only by hard begging that Mr.
Bingham obtained the sitting."

Stuart had not painted a heroic full-length since
he had mocked the Lord Chancellor of Ireland, and
his interest in doing such a picture now was inspired
not by his esthetic sense but by social and financial
pressure. At heart, he felt the mode silly, as his comments on David's portrait of Napoleon show: "How
delicately the lace is drawn! Did one ever see richer
satin? The ermine is wonderful in its finish. And, by
Jove, the thing has a head!"

Even the most temperate artist has difficulty execut-
ing well a painting in which he does not believe; Stuart was far from temperate. Combining his memory of
pictures he despised with imported engravings which
he thought of as trash, he worked out a composition
containing a vastly over-elegant chair bearing the seal
of the United States, the heavily carved leg of an

even more elegant table, beautifully bound books, three fat marble columns, a completely irrelevant mulberry curtain with gold cords, and a sunset sky embellished with a rainbow. Thus armed, he waited for the promised sittings.

"Sir," Washington wrote Stuart, on April 11, 1796, "I am under promise to Mrs. Bingham to sit for you tomorrow at nine o'clock, and wishing to know if it would be convenient for you that I should do so, and whether it would be at your house (as she talked of the State House), I send this note to you to seek information."

Wherever Stuart set up his easel, Washington appeared before it wearing a set of false teeth that pulled the lower part of his face out of shape. They fitted so badly that he used them for only a short time, but it was the time of the Lansdowne portrait. Not only did the distorted mouth bother Stuart; he was puzzled how to make the General's figure look heroic. He complained that Washington's "shoulders were high and narrow, his hands and feet remarkably large. He had aldermanic proportions, and this defect was increased by the form of the vest of that day."

Stuart mourned Washington's misshapen jaw, yet put it into the picture exactly as he saw it, although he knew this would mar the heroic effect toward which his composition was aimed. His motives are hard to analyze. The false teeth were a temporary blemish, and they could not be considered a primary indication of character. They revealed more about Washington's dentist than about Washington. And certainly Stuart was skillful enough to paint them out; to show the mouth as it had been when its own teeth held the lips firm and true. This would not have been considered flattery or faking by Stuart's contemporaries, but rather "realistic" as they defined realism.

According to the neo-classical point of view then dominant, it was a painter's duty to recognize and ignore "the accidents of nature," those chance configurations that would vanish in an hour or a decade; the painter was required to record a permanent, a "universal" image. Portraitists did not immortalize a man's hangover if he came to the studio too early in the morning, or even the pallor of a sickness that could be expected to pass. Three generations later, a school of painters was to shock Paris by trying to catch the fleeting moment, by depicting forms with an immediate rather than a generalizing vision. The Impressionists had a major fight on their hands before they could convince the connoisseurs that this was not humbug and idiocy.

That Stuart's adherence to the exact image before him at the moment of composition anticipated esthetic theories of the future did not mean that his conscious motivation was esthetic: it was probably documentary. When he painted lesser men than Washington, he was more inclined to seek an artistic synthesis. He may well have thought of his canvas as a record that would accompany the hero's fame down through the ages. Functioning as a historian, he should not edit or bowdlerize. And, amazingly, the public regretted the false teeth as Stuart had done, but did not ask him to paint them out. Parson Weems and his cherry tree were in the future. The Americans who had just won a war and established a republic felt the muse of history leaning over their shoulders, and they were neither ashamed nor afraid of what her cool gray eyes saw.

Perhaps Stuart was also swayed by a second motivation which he was not willing to admit even to himself. Proud but not really self-confident, he may well have resented the hero who was universally considered greater than he, who had embarrassed him at their first meeting, and who continued to treat him with the most frigid courtesy. There may have been anger behind the artist's depiction of that ill-shapen mouth.

Stuart entrusted many of the conventional background details, which struck him as so silly, to a signpainter and naïve portraitist, Jeremiah Paul. Paul, who was to shock Philadelphia by showing in a shopwindow his nude "Venus and Cupid, nine feet by seven,

taken from living models," possessed a flicker of wild
talent and a taste for liquor that rivaled Stuart's own.
We can visualize the two, a bottle between them,
laughing at the fat tassel that was appearing on the canvas, and then Stuart, with a sudden turn of mood, up-
braiding his assistant for lack of respect.

Also in the room would be an over-serious, red-
headed young man who, as he meticulously put
underpaint on unfinished parts of the huge picture,
tried to ignore the squabble. Descended from a line
of artisan painters in the Hudson River Valley, John
Vanderlyn had been working in a New York print
shop when he had met Stuart and had borrowed some
portraits to copy. One had been of Aaron Burr;
pleased with the result, Burr had placed Vanderlyn
with Stuart. Although his slow, humorless temperament contrasted with those of his mercuric studio-
mates, Vanderlyn, if his later work is any indication,
had no more sympathy than they with all the grandiloquent frippery that was being painted into the portrait.

Created for money in opposition to the esthetic
convictions of the artist and his assistants, the *Lansdowne Washington* was far from a masterpiece. However, the heroic representation of so great a man by
so famous a painter appeared to people who wished
to have an obviously splashy picture to show. Stuart

received many orders for copies, and since his usual pack of creditors was snapping at his heels, he accepted them. He found them hard to execute.

Before sailing to France as American minister, General Charles Cotesworth Pinckney paid Stuart five hundred dollars for a full-length to grace the embassy in Paris; it was never delivered. Timothy Pickering, United States Senator and former Secretary of State, wondered in 1804 whether the picture had ever been painted: "If it was, I think Stuart must have parted with it, intending doubtless to paint another for General Pinckney; but not having done it, gives no answer to his letters, because the explanation cannot be a pleasant one."

William Bingham sent Stuart's original full-length of Washington to Lord Lansdowne on October 29, 1796. Hoping to "rescue myself from pecuniary embarrassment and to provide for a numerous family at the close of an anxious life" by having the picture reproduced for the world market by an expert English engraver, Stuart, so he always insisted, had asked Bingham to stipulate that no unauthorized copy be made. Bingham agreed, but did not keep his agreement; the richest man in Philadelphia preferred to endanger the property of the impoverished artist rather than cheapen his gift by attaching strings. In all innocence, the British peer gave James Heath permission to reproduce the picture, remarking that Stuart would certainly be gratified at having his work engraved by an artist of such distinguished ability.

After Stuart told Bingham that he had commissioned West to find a suitable engraver, the banker finally acted, but even then only indirectly. On June 10, 1787 he wrote Rufus King, the American Ambassador in London, asking him to mention to Lansdowne Stuart's anxiety lest the picture be pirated. But much of a year had passed; the picture was already on copper.

Stuart wrote Lansdowne a courteous request for an explanation—what reply he received is not known—and called on Bingham in a fury. The banker, so the painter told his friends, asked whether he had any proof in writing of a promise to preserve the copyright. The artist, of course, had nothing in writing, for it had never occurred to him not to trust Bingham's word. He stamped out of the office, refusing to finish a picture of Mrs. Bingham he was painting, and thus banished himself forever from Philadelphia's leading salon.

In one of his famous anecdotes Stuart dramatized the arrival in America of the pirated engraving. For the purposes of this story, he claimed that he had been ignorant that the print was being made and that he was unknown in Dobson's Bookshop, on Philadelphia's Second Street. When he called there and expressed an interest in art, Dobson stated that a master-piece had just arrived from Europe and showed Stuart the guilty print. "Sir," Stuart cried, "the work is as infamous in execution as the motive that led to it."

"What? Have you the feelings of an American? What! Do you not respect the man here represented, nor the talents of the American painter who executed the original picture? What would Mr. Stuart say if he heard you speak thus?"

"It is my custom to speak the language of plainness and truth, whenever the character and fortune of any man are thus jeopardized. By this act, the family of the painter is ruined. My name is Stuart. I am the painter and have a right to speak." Stuart indicated what he thought every dealer should do by stating that Dobson nailed up the box that had just arrived from England, and never offered the print for sale.

The engraving was a most inferior one, and on every example the author of the original was given as "Gabriel Stuart." "They will make an angel of me despite myself," Stuart would say, but before his auditors had time to laugh he would be off on an impassioned complaint that he had never made a cent from the print, although it was an international best-seller. That he had violated his esthetic convictions to produce the best-seller only made the upshot more bitter. Efforts to find redress at law came to nothing. His daughters remembered how, as an old man, he would pace back and forth, gesticulating and muttering oaths, when the grievance came back to his memory. Indeed, he grew to blame all the financial difficulties which his improvidence had created on this one flagrant injustice.

Long before his quarrel with the Binghams, Stuart had found the gay society of the republican court annoying. Well-born loungers seemed to be knocking on his door all day long, demanding admittance when he wanted to paint, and they were outraged if he refused to see them. Nor did he find it easy to get on with his sitters, for the Federalist aristocrats regarded painters as drones, necessary to human vanity, perhaps, but hardly admirable. If artists were amusing and had a grand air as Stuart did, they might even be invited to the best parties, but no one for a moment considered them on the same level with merchants and generals and delicately nurtured females. When, some years later, the French sculptor M. Binon asked John Adams's advice on how to sell a bust portrait of Washington, the Federalist leader, who had been painted by West, Peale, Copley, and Stuart, replied:

Dear Sir,

I have received your polite favour of the third of this month. I am afraid you are engaged in speculation that will never be profitable to you. The age of paint-

ing and sculpture has not yet arrived in this country, and I hope it will not arrive very soon. Artists have done what they could with my face and eyes, head and shoulders, stature and figure, and they have made them monsters fit for exhibition as harlequin or clown. They may continue to do so as long as they please. I would not give sixpence for a picture of Raphael or a statue of Phidias. I am confident that you will not find purchasers for your bust, and therefore am sorry that you are engaged in so hopeless a speculation, because I believe you are a great artist and an admirable man.

> *I am, sir, with sincere esteem,*
> *Your most obt. humble servant,*
>
> *J. Adams*

Faced with such an attitude, Stuart carried his artistic arrogance to an extreme. After General Knox, Washington's first Secretary of War, had offended him, he used the General's portrait as the door for his pigsty. He refused to continue the picture of anyone who dared criticize the smallest detail; he would ring for his man and send the canvas up to the attic, nor could all the tears of a lady who needed a Stuart to enhance her social position make him change his mind. When "a gentleman of estimable character and no small consequence in his own eyes" objected that Stuart's portrait of the rich but homely widow he had married did not make her beautiful, the artist cried:

"What damned business is this of a portrait-painter! You bring him a potato and expect he will paint a peach."

Trott, the miniaturist, found him one day in a great fury. "That picture," he shouted, "has just been returned to me with the grievous complaint that the cravat is too coarse! Now, sir, I am determined to buy a piece of the finest texture, have it glued on the part that offends their exquisite judgment, and send it back." Once he delineated a handsome woman who was a great talker. When the picture was almost done, she looked at it and exclaimed: "Why, Mr. Stuart, you have painted me with my mouth open!"

"Madam, your mouth is always open," he replied, and refused to finish the picture.

Stuart's nerves had become dangerously tight. Shortly after completing the Lansdowne portrait, he moved to Germantown, a suburb of Philadelphia, where he installed his family at 5140 Main Street, in what was subsequently known as the Wister Mansion. Although he received few visitors, loneliness did not bring him quiet. "He has the appearance," an acquaintance wrote, "of a man who is attached to drinking, as his face is bloated and red." He created three hundred dollars' worth of portraits for a wine merchant whose taste for pictures was as strong as his own for Madeira, but found, when they balanced accounts, that he still owed two hundred dollars. He paid another liquor bill by painting the King of Prussia on horseback as a sign for Riter's Tavern.

"Mr. Stuart," writes Philadelphia's chronicler John Watson, "was noted for his eccentricity and his love of good eating and drinking. To the latter he was much addicted, showing therefrom a much inflamed face, and much recklessness in his actions when excited by his drink. In this he dealt in a wholesale way, buying his wine, brandy, and gin by the cask. On one occasion he was seen kicking a large piece of beef across the street from his house to Diehl's, his butcher." The meat, Stuart cried to the startled tradesman as he gave it a final placement through the door, was not fit to handle.

Dunlap was told that a journal Stuart kept in Germantown contained as a frequent notation, "Today quarreled with Tom." (Tom was his nickname for his wife.) Although not sure whether to believe this, Dunlap considered Stuart "undoubtedly an imprudent man, a bad husband and father." Trumbull wrote to Joseph Anthony, who was now a director of the Bank of the United States and richer than ever, "I am sorry to hear that Stuart still continues to be so great an enemy to himself. With his talents, poverty is a crime, as it can only be a consequence of idleness."

The engraver David Edwin, who visited him in Germantown, noted: "Mr. Stuart has been thought by many to have been harsh and repulsive in his man-

ners: to me he never appeared so." Giving credence
to one of Stuart's typical anecdotes, Edwin concluded
that his social difficulties were due to his taking seri-
ously the advice given him by the violent trial lawyer
and solicitor-general of England, Lord Edward Thur-
low: "If a man speaks disrespectfully of your art,
give him battle, my boy, give him battle!"

During February 1801 Stuart wished immediate
payment for a Washington portrait engaged by the
State of Connecticut; an installment, he explained,
was due on the "purchase of a small farm for my
family." Once more dreaming of solace in rural quiet,
he invested the proceeds from five whole-lengths of
Washington and twenty smaller pictures in the property near Pottsgrove, Pennsylvania, which he stocked
with imported Durham cows. He sent out the money
as fast as he received it, and neglected to take receipts.
When the man with whom he had been dealing died,
there was no evidence that he had ever paid a dollar;
he lost the whole sum, $3,442. Such lack of business
acumen contributed greatly to the debts with which
he was forever harassed. He could never remember
whether pictures had been paid for, and sometimes
enraged sitters by demanding his fee twice, or amazed
them by refusing sums due him. If he had money, he
was likely to mislay it; once he found a fifty-dollar bill
in a little-used pocket.

Yet he kept his reputation as the greatest painter in

America. When Mrs. Washington wanted a picture
of the President for herself, she persuaded her un-
willing husband to submit a third time to Stuart's
brush and company. In the stone barn he used as a
studio, the painter waited anxiously for Washington
to ride out for the first sitting, and sighed with relief
when he saw that the President's new false teeth did
not distort his face so much as the old. Washington
entered the barn with cold courtesy, sat down in the
chair Stuart had provided, and clamped his face into
the rigid expression he saved for portrait-painters.
Stuart plunged into his fund of anecdote, but the face
did not relax.

When Stuart looked up from his canvas after a
while, his heart almost stopped beating; Washington's
face bore a human expression. It lasted only a few
seconds, but by seemingly nonchalant questions Stuart
found out what had put it there; the General had seen
a noble horse gallop by the window. Instantly Stuart
commented on a local horse race; Washington made
an animated answer and his face came alive. Then
Stuart ransacked his mind for all he knew about
horses, and soon the two men were actually talking.
Stuart's brush flew merrily in rhythm with his tongue.
The conversation moved on to farming, a subject it
had never occurred to Stuart to discuss with a com-
mander-in-chief, and again Washington was interested.

Not too interested, however. Before the picture was finished, the President worked out a way to make the sittings bearable; he brought with him to the studio friends with whom he liked to talk: General Knox, with whom Stuart had not yet fought; the pretty Harriet Chew. They would keep his face alive, he dryly explained. Stuart at last saw the genial side of the hero, and he happened on an expedient to make the hero look imperial too, as if he were commanding an army. All Stuart had to do was be late for a sitting.

Stuart was delighted with the resulting picture. Although Washington had agreed to sit only so that his wife might have the portrait, Stuart determined to keep it; he felt he could make a fortune from copying it for all comers. He completed the face but not the background, and whenever Mrs. Washington sent for the picture, he apologetically explained that it was not finished. Finally she came in person, bringing the President along. When he fobbed her off with the same transparent excuse, she walked out in a huff. Stuart always insisted that Washington had not followed at once, but had whispered in his ear that he was to keep the portrait as long as he wished, since it was of such great advantage to him. An intimate of Washington's circle, however, reports that the President was very annoyed with Stuart; that he came several times to the studio, demanding the picture, and finally said in a curt manner: "Well, Mr. Stuart, I will not call again for this portrait. When it is finished, send it to me." The picture was never finished. Mrs. Washington had to put up with a copy, which she told her friends was not a good likeness.

Stuart's third picture of Washington, which shows the left side of his face, is known as the Athenaeum portrait, since it eventually came into the possession of the Boston Athenaeum. Whether it resembled the President or not, one thing is certain: it was immensely popular in its own day, and is the only representation of the father of their country which most modern Americans know. Stuart himself ceased using his other two portraits; he destroyed, or so he said, the original of the Vaughan type, and topped his copies of the Lansdowne full-length with the Athenaeum head. He kept the canvas by him all his life and, whenever his creditors became too importunate, dashed off copies to which he gaily referred as his "hundred-dollar bills." He sold more than seventy, and could have sold many more.

Stuart's nerves were not quieted by the tendency of other painters to do a rushing business in copying his copies, either openly or with the intention of making forgeries. An enterprising merchant even had some imitations run up in Canton, China, forcing the artist into a lawsuit.

Dunlap tells the following story in what purport to be Stuart's words: "When I lived in Germantown, a

little, pert man called and addressed me thus: 'You
are Mr. Stuart, the great painter?'

" 'My name is Stuart, sir.'

" 'My name is Winstanley, sir; you must have
heard of me.'

" 'Not that I recollect, sir.'

" 'No! Well, Mr. Stuart, I have been copying
your full-length of Washington; I have made a number of copies; I have now six that I have brought on
to Philadelphia; I have got a room in the State House;
and I have put them up; but before I show them to
the public and offer them for sale, I have a proposal
to make to you.'

" 'Go on, sir.'

" 'It would enhance their value, you know, if I
could say that you had given them the last touch.
Now, sir, all you have to do is to ride to town and
give each of them a tap, you know, with your riding-
switch—just thus, you know. And we will share the
amount of the sale.'

" 'Did you ever hear that I was a swindler?'

" 'Sir! Oh, you mistake. You know—'

" 'You will please to walk downstairs, sir, very
quickly, or I shall throw you out the window.' "

When the burly painter laid down his snuffbox
and prepared for action, Winstanley decided he preferred the stairs.

Stuart asserted that even the full-length which

adorned the White House was one of Winstanley's forgeries. However, that was not the common opinion, and the mystical importance that was ascribed to Stuart's *Washingtons* even during the artist's lifetime is shown by the care which was taken to save the picture when the English took the capital in 1814. As she fled, Dolly Madison, the President's wife, commanded a servant to save or destroy "the portrait of President Washington, the eagles which ornament the drawing-room, and the four cases of papers which you will find in the President's private room. The portrait I am very anxious to save, as it is the only original by Stuart. In all events, don't let them fall into the hands of the enemy, as their capture would enable them to make a great flourish."

Stuart's three life paintings of Washington were not among his best works, for he had undertaken what was for him an impossible task. He had tried to make votive canvases before which multitudes would fall down in worship; yet his own stubborn spirit was incapable of worship. Even the most delicate-fingered phrenologist could have found no bump of reverence on that fierce old head.

Although a version of the Lansdowne portrait was bought in 1947 by the Brooklyn Museum for seventy thousand dollars, the full-lengths are dreadful pictures, stilted, unperspicacious, dull. The Athenaeum portrait has a cameolike perfection that shows up well on postage stamps, yet it reveals little of that profound insight into character which is the glory of Stuart's greatest pictures. Of the three life portraits, critics usually prefer the more rough-hewn and less idealized Vaughan portrait, but even it leaves the serious student of either art or human nature much to wish for.

The General's associates were by no means unanimous in preferring Stuart's likeness of Washington to those by some of the other artists for whom the suffering hero sat. Certain it is that Stuart worked under a great disadvantage, for by 1790 Washington's splendid physique had begun to break down. The dashing commander of Revolutionary days was a tired old man, who had been drafted for the Presidency against his will. He complained that every act of his administration had been grossly misrepresented, "and that too in such exaggerated and indecent terms as could scarcely be applied to Nero, a notorious defaulter, or even a common pickpocket." He was very sad. When Stuart had tried, by talking of battles, to make Washington look as he had looked at Valley Forge, he had tried the impossible; it was a different man who sat before him. Undoubtedly Trumbull and Charles Willson Peale, who had painted Washington many years before, had enjoyed a better opportunity to show him at his best, though they were less expert portraitists.

Stuart himself did not contend that his rendering of Washington was pre-eminent. "Houdin's bust," he told his daughter, "came first, and my head next. When I painted him, he had just had a set of false teeth inserted, which accounts for the constrained expression about his mouth and the lower part of his face. Houdon's bust [done in 1783] did not suffer from this defect."

Although Stuart's *Washingtons* have made his name a national byword, they have done great damage to his artistic reputation. His copies of his Athenaeum portrait, which for patriotic reasons occupy prominent positions in so many museums, are for the most part vastly inferior to the original: some of the faces, indeed, seem hardly human. Impetuous and actuated by inspiration, Stuart was not able to imitate anyone successfully, not even himself. As the years passed, he kept altering, perhaps unconsciously, the shape of Washington's head; at first he made it shorter and squatter than in his original painting; then he went too far the other way and turned out a series of heads that were longer and thinner. Finally he became so bored that his *Washingtons* were merely superficial sketches of the features he had painted *ad nauseum*. "Mr. Stuart," Neagle wrote, "told me one day when we were before this original portrait that he could never make a copy of it to satisfy himself, and that at last, having made so many, he worked mechanically and with little interest." His daughter remembered that toward the end of his life Stuart dashed off *Washingtons* at the rate of one every two hours.

CHAPTER NINE

FAME WITHOUT FORTUNE

WITH the collapse of Federalist control and the inauguration of Jefferson, the national capital was moved to the District of Columbia. Three years later, in 1803, Stuart followed. His Philadelphia affairs proved so entangled that before he could leave he had to put them in the hands of a broker, Edward Stow. Not sure he would stay in the new city of Washington, he settled his family at Bordentown, New Jersey.

The money Stuart had left with his wife was soon exhausted, but no further sums came from her husband. On December 22, sixteen-year-old Charles Gilbert Stuart wrote Stow: "Send me the gun as soon as you can, as vacation has commenced, which is only one week, and the greatest service you can now do me would be to send me some powder and shot, be it ever so little, as Mama's circumstances are such at present as to be unable to let me have any money."

Word came to Bordentown that Stuart was in full employ at Washington, yet his wife, his son, his three daughters, and whatever short-lived baby whimpered in the nursery sank ever closer to starvation. Stow was finally accused of keeping for himself money that Stuart had sent his family. The broker complained to the painter, and on May 15, 1804 Stuart finally got around to writing one of his extremely rare letters:

"Nothing could give me more surprise and concern than to find that any censure should reach so sincere and disinterested a friend as I have on all occasion found you. But I feel the utmost indignation that should be found a being so base and impudent as to attack the character of my friend in the most tender point, and to make me an instrument for such a purpose. Truth, my dear friend, is simple but powerful, and I know no way to repel so infamous an attack as by stating it.

"First then—I never did until the present moment direct to you or to your care any letters containing money for the use of my family nor for any other purpose. . . . That there were three letters, of which I obtained no account, containing money—forty dollars each. They were directed to Mrs. Stuart at Bordentown, but they never reached the post office, which is about two miles from my lodging. The weather being severe, the idle rascal who I had entrusted them to had concealed them in his own box. Thus, sir, I hope I have removed entirely anything that could give either of us uneasiness."

Stuart enclosed a hundred dollars, promised to send another hundred the next day and still another the day following. The money was to be used to return a loan to a Mr. Franks, otherwise unidentified, and to meet the grocer's bill with Boller and Johnson which Stuart had been unable to pay when he left Pennsylvania. "This sum is more than sufficient for these debts, as I must insist on the deducting one hundred dollars, which is the price of the head of Washington which has been spoiled by Franks making a hole through it. Should any difficulty arise on this subject, Mr. [Alexander James] Dallas [the Secretary of the Treasury] or Mr. [Joseph] Hopkinson [Congressman and jurist] will, I am certain, give you their advice cheerfully on my account. I must beg you to make my best thanks to Messrs. Boller and Jordan for their kind indulgence to me."

Stuart had set up his Washington studio on F Street, near Seventh. "I can tell you nothing new," a friend wrote to Dolly Madison. "Stuart is all the rage. He is almost worked to death and everyone is afraid they will be the last to be finished. He says: 'The ladies come to me and say: "*Dear* Mr. Stuart, I'm afraid you must be very tired. You really must rest when *my* picture is done." ' "

During a trip to Baltimore, Stuart began portraits of Jerome Bonaparte, Napoleon's favorite brother, and his American bride, but when Jerome condescended to him in the proper princely manner, Stuart slammed down his brushes and refused to finish the pictures. Years later his pupil Thomas Sully accidentally stepped on a canvas tossed onto the floor of Stuart's lumber room. "You needn't mind," said Stuart. "It's only a damned French barber." Sully remembers that "Stuart had a beautiful picture of Jerome's beautiful wife, which he refused to give up, threatening that if he was bothered any more about it, he would put rings through the nose and send it to any tavern-keeper who would hang it up. He would have done it too, for he was not a man to flinch from anything of that kind."

When he was painting Dolly Madison's sister, Mrs. Anna Cutts, the lively young woman got into an argument with him about what features were most expressive of character; she supported the eyes and mouth, Stuart was for the nose. Before the next sitting, he painted into the background of her portrait a brownish column, the base of which jutted out like his own chin, and a green curtain protruding halfway across the picture and draped into a caricature of his own tremendous nose. The joke having evoked the laughter of his sitter, Stuart prepared to paint it out, but she would not let him. It is a final proof of how suave was Stuart's style that the comic profile is so assimilated into the composition that it in no way detracts from the over-all effect.

Whatever Mrs. Stuart may have thought of her husband, the ladies of Washington found him greatly entertaining. In June 1804 Mrs. Madison wrote Mrs. Cutts that he "has now nearly finished all his portraits and says he means to go directly to Boston, but that is what he has said these two years; being a man of genius, he of course does things differently from other people. I hope he will be here next winter, as he has bought a square to build a 'temple' upon."

Stuart did spend the next winter in Washington, but in the spring of 1805 he finally succumbed to the persuasion of the Massachusetts Senator, Jonathan Mason. Having visited his family at Bordentown, he proceeded alone to Boston, where he stayed at Champotin's Hotel on Summer Street. "I saw him there," wrote Dunlap, "both in the painting-room and at the dinner table. His mornings were passed in the first, and too much of the remainder of the day in the second." He was forced to borrow money from a merchant, Thomas L. Winthrop, to establish himself, but soon he had, in the words of the miniaturist Charles Fraser, "all the beauty and talent of Boston under his pencil." Delighted with his prospects, he took a house on Washington Street to which he brought his family.

Political controversy soon raged around him. "Samuel Parkman, Esq.," the *Boston Columbian Centinel* reported on March 5, 1806, "has presented to this town an elegant full-length portrait of the immortal Washington, copied from the painting of the celebrated Stuart, with a request that it may be placed in a conspicuous part of Faneuil Hall, when the [restoration of the historic] hall is completed, which will be by June next."

Parkman, a prominent Federalist merchant, made the actual presentation at a Town Meeting on March 10. The Federalists applauded the picture, but a Jeffersonian, the stucco-worker Joseph Baston, "expressed my dissatisfaction with it." He demanded an original painting: a mere copy, he stated, was unworthy of the community. This produced cheers from the Jeffersonians, and an angry retort from the moderator that Baston should "never be employed as a mechanic in the town of Boston again." The meeting adjourned until the twelfth.

On that date the Federalists used parliamentary procedure and abuse to silence Baston. "I had determined to express myself more fully on the subject," he wrote, "but this was disagreeable to the moderator, and still more to the paper skull of Mr. [Ebenezer] Clough [a paper-manufacturer], who insisted that foreigners had no business to come there 'bull-ragging,' as he called it." Moving his "bull-ragging" to the press, Baston stated that the Washington portrait was one of the unauthorized copies which Winstanley had painted and then, when they did not sell, had tried to legitimize by asking Stuart to touch them with his riding-crop. After his dash for safety down Stuart's studio steps, Winstanley had sent two of the copies to the West Indies, but even in this distant market they found no purchasers. They were returned, attached for freight, and finally sold at an auction, where Parkman had picked up what the Federalists had been booming as a munificent gift. "It is certainly not to the credit of Faneuil Hall," Baston concluded, "to be decorated with a picture, a stolen copy by a foreigner from the celebrated Stewart [sic], who is at this time in this town, and is the only man who ever took a correct likeness of Washington."

The effect of this disclosure, Stuart told Dunlap, "was electrical and spread through the town." Ragged Jeffersonian urchins ran hooting behind Parkman's well-appointed carriage; the Federalist aristocracy were besieged by a wave of vulgar mirth. Finally, retreat was decided upon; Parkman was advised to buy from Stuart an authentic full-length of Washington for presentation to the city.

"How much will it cost?" Stuart quoted him as asking ruefully.

"Six hundred dollars, perhaps."

"Five and six are eleven," Parkman objected, thinking of what he had already paid for the Winstanley copy.

"Something must be done, and quickly."

"But how can I call on Mr. Stuart after this affair?"

"We will negotiate the matter."

A delegation, including Isaac P. Davis, the rich

merchant who was Stuart's most intimate patron, called on him. When it was explained that the picture would have to be an obviously dazzling one, and would have to be run up quickly—the new presentation was scheduled for July 4—the painter proved for once co-operative. He even agreed to make his nearest approach to the historical style he had shied away from in West's studio. Washington was to be shown as a general, standing at Dorchester Heights under a sky dark with cannon smoke, bright with cannon flash. The suggestion that a horse be included must have momentarily taken Stuart back, for he knew he was no animal-painter, but Davis's offer to have a steed brought to his studio may have touched his risibilities, and it occurred to him to simplify the problem by having the horse stand with his rump to the spectator in a manner that made foreshortening unnecessary.

The composition decided upon, Stuart dashed off the huge canvas—ten feet by seven—in nine days. It has been pointed out that the horse is the most wooden since Troy, and indeed *Washington at Dorchester Heights* is one of Stuart's least successful pictures. Nor was it as financially rewarding as he had hoped. He complained to Dunlap that Parkman "paid me in undercurrent banknotes which I had to send to a broker to be exchanged."

Although Stuart had hurried to the rescue of the

Federalists, he was not their convinced partisan. He had undoubtedly regretted the diminution, when the Jeffersonians came into power, of that Georgian elegance which appealed to one side of his temperament, yet the Republican leaders had treated him with less arrogance than their predecessors. Unlike Washington, who had shown him only the most formal courtesy, Jefferson had invited him to stay at Monticello if he ever visited Virginia; Dolly Madison, the Republican hostess, had been his constant friend, never stabbing him in the back the way the Binghams had done.

As his departure to England at the outbreak of the Revolution had indicated, politics seemed of so little importance to him that it was one of the few directions in which he was willing to compromise for worldly advantage. He cultivated the Bostonians most able to pay his fees; the majority were Federalists. Yet he did not commit himself to their party as long as it remained possible to take no stand. Waterhouse, who was a leader of the local Jeffersonians, writes that Stuart "vindicated me at the dinner and supper tables" of the conservatives "amidst their toasts and insults." However, when the War of 1812 fanned the outrage of the New England aristocracy into plans for secession from the Union, "the current ran so strong that Stuart thought it to his interest to yield to it." This caused a second break between the boyhood cronies.

Although Stuart was always fighting with someone, he lived in a sea of people, as a journal he kept
in 1808 reveals. Here are entries for two typical days
—Monday, April 25, and Wednesday, April 27—
with the first names of persons added whenever they
can be ascertained with any chance of correctness.
The meaning of the X's and numbers Stuart included
is not clear.

M. 25 Miss Charlotte
Morton } *Disappointed me*   11
Miss Caroline Knox

Rubbed in Mrs. [John Clarke] Howard's and Mrs.
[Benjamin] Bussy's background

Rubbed in Col. [Isaac P.] Davis' drapery

State Street altered, Mr. [Nathan] Appleton's en-
gagement. Mr. and Mrs. [Patrick] Grant, with a lady
and gentleman from N.Y.

Caught in the rain at Seymour's [Furniture] Ware-
house.

W. 27 Col. Boyd, Mr. [Samuel] Dexter and Miss
E. Morton   X   11

Mr. T[homas] H[andasyd] Perkins   X   Dr. [Sam-
uel] Danforth, Mr. [James] Greenleaf   X

Mr. McGee—Mrs. Morton—Mr. [Jeremiah] Allen
with a British officer—State Street—walked in the
Mall with H[enry] Sargent [a painter]—Dr. Dix's
house

Mrs. [Anne Catherine] Powell and Miss [Julia Maria] Murray X *—Stackpole and Gay* X *—Mr. [Ralph] Shaw evening is to tune my harpsichord.*

Stuart's love of music was as strong as ever. Sully praised "his execution on an organized pianoforte very highly," and another visitor reported that he had a small organ on which he "played several old-fashioned tunes with much feeling and execution." To cater to this passion was the best avenue to his good graces. "I called to see Mr. Stewart," a Boston matron, Mrs. Charles Davis, wrote in 1809. "Found him in one of his happiest humors, and with a little flattery, which we all like at times (and a song Catherine had copied for him), we made him promise to have my father's [Benjamin Bussy's] portrait finished in a month from this time. I told him I should pursue him like his own shadow until he completed it."

Boston gossip, as reported by an aunt to Stuart's old disciple Mather Brown, dwelt eternally on the number of pictures he had in his studio unfinished. The rumor ran that it took Stuart three years to finish a portrait: "He is indeed very eccentric. He loves a cheerful bottle and does no work in the afternoon. He is very dilatory. . . . There is no economy, of course. He is said to be poor."

For no apparent reason, Stuart refused lucrative

commissions. Although the fifteen thousand dollars which the Pennsylvania Academy of the Fine Arts offered him for a copy of the *Lansdowne Washington* was more than he had received for the original, he never answered their letter. When New York City asked him to paint full-lengths of heroes of the War of 1812, he did start one of Isaac Hull. Months passed with no further word of the picture. Finally Sully, guessing at the trouble and grateful to Stuart for instruction, offered to paint in the details, draperies, and accessories. His letter also was not answered.

John Quincy Adams wrote Copley in 1811 that Stuart had agreed to make a portrait of John Adams for the legislature of Massachusetts: "He actually took a likeness of the face. But Mr. Stuart thinks it the prerogative of genius to disdain the performance of engagements, and he did disdain the performance of that."

The Roman Catholics of Boston offered Stuart two hundred dollars to paint the Reverend Dr. Taylor of the Ursaline Convent in Charlestown. Stuart delivered a picture he had not bothered to finish and demanded three hundred dollars. Only when the Catholics refused to give him a cent did he amend the canvas, making it "a fine one." Dunlap, who received this anecdote from Stuart's friend, the journalist Samuel L. Knapp, commented that Knapp and Stuart's pupil James Frothingham agreed that the great artist was "a passionate man and a great liar."

In a biographical sketch he himself published, Knapp attributed Stuart's faults to "irritable nerves and delicate fibres: . . . diseases of the physical nature."

Knapp noted that if one of "the choice spirits who surrounded him" dared hint at a defect in a portrait, Stuart would resent it, even if he made the improvement: but he saved his real fury for sitters. Should a member of the public, however exalted his station, offer even the mildest suggestion, Stuart parried the first attempts with delicate sarcasm or a sneer; then he turned on his patron "with that appalling directness that either produces silence or a quarrel."

Stuart, Knapp continued, had no respect for the ordinary business of life and the people who transacted it; he mocked the conventional virtues of prudence and thrift, reserving his admiration for "commanding talents in literature and art." Nor did all kinds of artists meet with his approval. He despised painters who became skillful through hard work rather than brilliance. Copley, Stuart remarked, put more labor into a hand than he himself did into a whole picture, which only resulted in making Copley's flesh tones look like "tanned leather." In examining pictures, Stuart sought signs of genius. A man, he said, should not try to "come among the prophets" unless he was touched with divine fire.

"Stuart's word in the art is law," wrote John Neal, "and from his decision there is no appeal." When Washington Allston, America's first truly romantic painter, settled in Boston after a brilliant European career, even he deferred to Stuart. Allston had brought with him from London a huge Biblical canvas, *Belshazzar's Feast*, which was almost finished. So great was his reputation that the American connoisseurs could hardly wait for the exhibition of what was already known as "The Great Picture." Given a private view, Stuart made a devastating criticism. The younger artist started to repaint. It was the tragedy of Allston's life, and one of the strangest stories in the annals of American art, that he was never again able to bring near to completion this picture for which the public clamored eagerly and with growing puzzlement decade after decade. Allston became so sensitive about his failure that he made workmen whom he was forced to admit to his studio walk backward lest they glimpse even a corner of the vast canvas. Not till after Allston's death in 1843 did any eyes but the painter's own see what he had achieved. Then a committee of Boston's leading intellectuals tiptoed into the empty room, pulled back the curtain, and were confronted with a confused and pitiful wreck. The principal figure had been blotted out with a covering of dark-brown paint. "That," said Richard Henry Dana, Sr., "is his shroud."

Although Stuart's criticism had started off this descending spiral, it was, of course, only one of many factors that produced the tragedy. Prophesying that the picture would never be completed, Stuart had explained that Allston's mind grew so rapidly "that the work of this month or year was felt to be imperfect the next, and must be done over and over again or greatly altered, and therefore could never come to an end." Yet it is significant that this younger man, who worked in a different style and was himself to become in turn the artistic dictator of Boston, was so impressed by Stuart that a word from the aging portrait-painter could throw him from the highroad into the underbrush of endlessly unsatisfied experimentation.

Allston and Sully once examined a Stuart portrait together. "I may commit myself and expose my ignorance," said Sully, "but, in my opinion, I never saw a Rembrandt, Rubens, Van Dyck, or Titian to equal it."

Allston replied: "I say all combined never equaled it."

Such adulation encouraged Stuart to paint exactly as he pleased. Making with increasing reluctance any concessions to the international portrait style, he concentrated on depicting character in faces, and tended to throw everything else overboard. Although he could still reveal laces and fabrics and jewels expertly, with a few quick strokes of the brush, he usually did not bother. He was able to carry his brilliance over into a territory from which brilliance is often out-lawed: into extreme simplicity. When painting the wealthy merchant David Sears, he placed the figure asymmetrically on the canvas, the swell of the body to the left justifying the position of the head. The rough contour of the young man's curly hair echoes the out-line of the crisply painted ruffle on the breast. A gray background shading to brown shows off delightfully the hair's chestnut hue, the flesh tints, the white linen, the black coat. This is a beautiful picture, finished in every detail, and furthermore it satisfies to perfection Stuart's ideal of emphasizing not accessories but the likeness itself.

Too often during his Boston period he lacked the patience to create such well-rounded and thought-out pictures. After he had painted the features carefully, he added the body any old way, in a dash of irrita-tion. Or he entrusted it to an assistant. Among his most impressive later pictures are several he aban-doned before they were completed. *Washington All-ston* is an example: the quick, profound rendition of the over-sensitive face is surrounded with black can-vas, which, although it does not add to the image, does not detract as a carelessly executed torso and background would have done.

At Boston, as in Philadelphia, Stuart's favorite drapery-painter shared his own wild temperament. He was so fond of John Ritto Penniman that he allowed the young man to make a tracing of his most valuable asset, the *Athenaeum Washington*. An ornamental painter normally dedicated to signs and militia banners, Penniman would tackle anything: a landscape, six feet by three, for the Columbian Lodge; a tremendous *Last Supper*. What the *Boston Saturday Evening Globe* called "the eccentricities of genius" brought him at last to bankruptcy, and he served time in prison.

Stuart also relied for assistance on the beginners who called at his studio, begging instruction. Since there was no art school in the United States that adequately taught painting, the knocks on his door were frequent. He demanded that each caller bring him a sample picture, or, if far from home, paint one for him to see. His object, as he explained to the Pennsylvania-Dutch tinware-decorator Jacob Eichholtz, was to make sure his visitor was "not an impostor." Tinware-decorators who could record an image were welcome, but he had no use for polite young men who aspired to paint but had never painted.

A Massachusetts chaise-maker, James Frothingham, walked many miles to Stuart's studio carrying one of his early crude efforts at portraiture. When within sight of the house, he hid the canvas and, so he later remembered, paced irresolutely. At last he rushed to the door and knocked. He was about to flee, but the door opened.

"Your name, sir, and I will introduce you."

Frothingham mumbled his name. With horrifying speed, he was ushered into Stuart's presence.

Stuart looked up from his painting, angry at the interruption, but when he saw the terrified young man and guessed his errand, a gentle look came on the lion-like face that was so rarely gentle. Having waited patiently for Frothingham to find his tongue and state his needs, Stuart said: "I will tell you anything I know. Have you brought a specimen of your skill?"

"I brought a portrait, sir. It is out of doors."

"Bring it in, sir. We do not turn pictures out of doors here. Bring it in."

Stuart put the picture on an easel next to one of his own, and then asked what was Frothingham's present employment.

"Coach-painting, sir."

"Stick to it! You had better be a tea-waterman's horse in New York than a portrait-painter anywhere." But Stuart made it clear that he was criticizing the economics of art, not the ability of the beginner. Frothingham went off the possessor of much advice and encouragement. Every time he finished a new portrait, he walked it over to Stuart for criticism, and when he came in with his sixth, Stuart exclaimed: "You do not know how well you have done this!"

William Peckham, a soldier stationed in Boston harbor who was to become a portrait-painter in Indiana, dropped in on Stuart during 1810. He was, so he wrote his father, "somewhat surprised at finding a man who seems to be so anxious for my improvement." Stuart promised "all the information in the art of painting gratis," and "a seat in his room as often as I shall call on him. He has given me a very fine piece of cloth, and offers me pencils and paints."

When Thomas Sully visited Boston in 1807, he was already a portraitist of reputation who had emerged from the primitive ranks, and his temperament was opposite to Stuart's. (He was soon to succumb to that fanciest of influences, Sir Thomas Lawrence.) Yet he wrote that "the privilege of standing by the artist's chair during a sitting was a situation I valued more, at that moment, than I shall ever appreciate any station on earth." Before the sitting was over, Isaac P. Davis happened in. It was agreed that Sully should paint Stuart's principal patron so that Stuart would have a portrait to criticize. Although Sully saw Stuart only occasionally over a period of three weeks, it took a trip to Europe to divorce him completely from the powerful influence that was so unsuited to his natural style.

The only beginner Stuart failed to impress was, as far as we know, his nephew and namesake, Gilbert Stuart Newton. On his arrival in Boston, Stuart had found all the surviving members of his immediate family in residence there. His father, who had abandoned the Nova Scotia farm for a snuff mill at Halifax, had died in 1793; his mother had gone to live with her daughter Ann, who was married to Henry Newton, the Halifax collector of customs. But Newton died in 1802, and the two widows moved, with Ann's children, to Boston, where Ann established a girls' school.

Exhibiting a taste for painting, Gilbert Stuart Newton was from the age of ten given the run of his uncle's studio. However, he proved no more amenable to instruction than his elder had been when a youth. After the two males had had a squabble, Mrs. Stuart tried to smooth things over by asking her husband if he did not think Newton possessed "fine talents."

"Undoubtedly he has," Stuart replied, "but he is such a consummate coxcomb I have no patience with him. If I attempt to instruct him, he invariably contradicts me."

A showdown came when Newton, especially pleased with a fine stroke on a picture he was painting, rushed into his uncle's room, flourished his brush, and cried: "Now, old gentleman, I'll teach you to paint!"

"You'll teach me to paint, will you? I'll teach you

manners." And not happening to have gout that day, Stuart kicked him out of the room.

Newton found his way to Europe. He talked against his uncle, but behaved in the true Stuart manner by refusing to walk any well-trod path: he scorned to be a historical painter; he did not wish to be a portraitist. He became a genre painter and, after he settled in London, created some of the nineteenth century's earliest impressive scenes of domestic life. Although Newton died insane at the age forty-one, he has a secure if small niche in the history of art.

Stuart's favorite pupil was Matthew Harris Jouett, whom he called "Kentucky" for it was from that state, then in the extreme West, that the young man appeared in 1816. He was on his way to Europe, but Stuart, who twenty years before had urged Vanderlyn to complete his education abroad, warned Jouett to stay home lest his style be ruined. European painting, he now believed, was "at a standstill" because pictures were compared to old masters, not, as in the United States, to nature.

When rich Bostonians talked of starting an art academy, Stuart killed the project with his powerful opposition. Trustees of such institutions, he explained, had more money than taste, and as for formal instruction, it merely encouraged the incompetent. "Bye and bye," he shouted, "you will not by any chance kick your foot against a dog kennel but out will start a portrait-painter." Stuart foresaw modern conditions under which you cannot by any chance step on a young lady's toe at a debutante party but "ouch" will be said by a writer or painter.

Stuart believed that artists should draw their own conclusions directly from nature, and he urged this on his pupils, forgetting that he himself had been forced by failure to study in West's studio. He was worried when he found his disciples examining his own pictures—"Oh, my boy," he cried to Neagle, "you should not do that!"—but a notebook kept by Jouett during his four months with Stuart reveals that in practice his method of instruction was to show the young what he himself did. In explaining how he constructed a head, he asked his pupils to imagine a face reflected back and forth between a series of mirrors. First you placed on canvas the vague form seen in the third mirror. Then you turned to the second mirror; the features became clearer, but were still blurred. Finally you achieved the image in the first mirror, where everything was clear and sharp.

This method of building up forms was revolutionary in a day when painting was regarded as a gaudy annex to the purer palace of draftsmanship. Students in conventional studios were not permitted to pick up a brush until they were expert at line drawing; critics admired in particular correctness of outline. As late as

1859, canvases by Whistler and Manet were rejected for the Paris Salon because, in the words of the modern critic John Rewald, "they were conceived as harmonies of masses modeled in color without the aid of line." Not until the 1870's did the Impressionists succeed in overthrowing the linear preconception which had dominated European art for centuries.

However, Stuart only partially realized his originality. He told Jouett that he dispensed with line drawings because you could draw better with oil paint on a brush, and he repeated the neo-classical doctrine he had imbibed years before in West's studio: "Coloring is not so significant to us as drawing, and as it partakes more of common mechanical employment—in a word, is more closely allied to matter than intelligence—so 'tis inferior to design. . . . Raphael, who was a bad colorist, for his great invention, composition, expression, and design has been called 'the Divine,' whereas Titian [and] Corregio, who [were] the great colorists, [have] a reputation of limited extent."

Actually, color was Stuart's principal tool. Flesh, he told Jouett, "is like no other substance under heaven. It has all the gaiety of a silk-mercer's shop without its gaudiness and gloss, and all to the soberness of old mahogany without its sadness." Neagle recorded Stuart's statement that "good flesh partook of all colors, not mixed so as to combine into one tint, but shining through each other, like blood through the natural skin."

In order to give flesh tones depth and texture, Stuart usually blocked in the face with opaque pigments, which he then covered with a swiftly painted layer of transparent or semi-transparent hues. This technique enabled him to paint faces with the dash and spontaneity which during his English years he had reserved for backgrounds. At last he could have created a complicated picture in a single, unified style, but he was no longer interested.

Neagle reports: "He deliberated every time before the well-charged brush went down upon the canvas with an action like cutting into it with a knife. He lifted the brush from the surface at a right angle, carefully avoiding a sliding motion. He always seemed to avoid vexing or tormenting the paint when once laid on, and this accounts partly for the purity and freshness . . . of his work."

Stuart himself told Jouett: "Preserve as far as practicable the round, blunt stroke in preference to the winding, flirting, whisping manner. . . . Never be sparing of color, load your pictures, but keep your colors as separate as you can. No blending, 'tis destructive of clear and beautiful effect. It takes [away from] the transparency and liquidity of coloring, and renders the flesh the consistency of buckskin." He added that the academic manner of his master, Benjamin West, made flesh look "wormy."

Since Stuart laid his colors side by side, his pictures looked best from a slight distance. When people examined them closely, he would cry in anger: "Does it smell good?"

Although Stuart's method of putting on pigment in separate dots seems to foreshadow the Impressionists, his object was very different. Far from using contrasting hues that were to be mixed by the eye of the observer, Stuart juxtaposed colors that shaded from each other only a little. He denied another principle of the Impressionists when he stated: "My idea is as little colors in the shadows as you can."

Stuart's painting-methods were too personal to communicate to anyone else, too sophisticated to sink deep into the minds of the ingenious artisans who flocked to his studio. Those of his pupils who went furthest sought further instruction: Sully sat at the feet of Sir Thomas Lawrence; Vanderlyn imbibed the neo-classicism of Napoleon's Paris; Newton was less moved by his uncle's example than by that of the Dutch masters. Jouett and Frothingham, who most accurately reproduced Stuart's style, translated his lyrical visions into a somewhat inept prose.

The revolt Stuart sparked against aristocratic portrait conceptions was more widely applicable. Anyone could banish elegant costumes and accessories from the foregrounds of pictures, and from the backgrounds, columns, curtains, and decorative vistas. Ignoring the fact that it took great skill to make such pictures esthetically interesting, Stuart's disciples concentrated on analyzing personalities against unrepresentational graduations of color. Such images were so suited to the basic thinking of American democracy that they spread far beyond the circle of Stuart's firsthand contacts to dominate, for better or worse, a full generation of American portrait-painters.

CHAPTER TEN

ON DESPERATE SEAS

OLD age, which he had pitied in others, now bore down on Stuart too. Trying to forget the flaws and deficiencies of his own temperament, the unhappiness of his own career, he concentrated his hopes for the future on his son, Charles Gilbert Stuart, who he felt had great talent as a landscapist. But he was so afraid of destroying the lad's originality that he refused to give him any instruction. Charles Gilbert was forced to appeal to Stuart's other pupils for hints at second hand.

From the beginning, Stuart had been worried about his son, who seemed to be so like himself; in the tantrums of the infant he had seen his own unstable nerves. Realizing that he had wasted much of his own life, he determined to save his son from the pitfalls into which he himself had fallen. He brought Charles Gilbert up with savage strictness. When the boy did things he saw his father do every day, his father recognized the symptoms he dreaded and flew into a fury. The years passed with much sternness and many beatings, until at last the young man could be controlled no longer. Then he threw himself into dissipation with more abandon than his father had ever known. Stuart sat up many a night till dawn, waiting for the front door to open, and when at last the prodigal returned, pale, feverish, so drunk he could hardly stand, the old man wondered if this could be retribution.

The boy who was so like Stuart himself, so talented, so uncontrolled, did complete at least two pictures, *A Buffalo Hunt* and *A Poacher*, that were lent to the Boston Athenaeum years later. For the rest, he wasted away under the influence of liquor and late hours. While his father watched in anguished helplessness, he grew thinner, more drawn, till he could hardly stagger to the haunts of his companions. Finally, he was too weak to get out of bed; Charles Gilbert died on March 10, 1813, at the age of twenty-six. Although the official record gave the cause of death as consumption, Stuart felt that dissipation had killed his favorite child, and that it was all his own fault. The sad expression of his face grew sadder.

The poverty his own recklessness had caused forced the father to bury his only son in the strangers' tomb of Trinity Church; the funeral procession consisted of only one carriage. Unable to bear the house in which Charles Gilbert had died, Stuart moved from Boston to suburban Roxbury. He inhabited a large, square structure just beyond Shawmut Avenue and tried, as of old, to find peace in the slow growth, the abundance of nature. He insisted on having cows and pigs.

The most childish things amused him now. An

irascible servant, for instance, got into such a fury with a cow that Molly clambered somehow up the barn stairs; the next morning everyone was amazed to see her head sticking out of the upper window. "This," comments one of his daughters, "was just the kind of thing to divert Stuart." He made his friends come out from Boston to see the cow, and was so amused that it took weeks of persuasion from his wife and daughters before he would let Molly be brought down to earth.

He delighted in infantile puns. "Mr. Stuart," a gushing lady would cry, "that is the greatest likeness I ever saw!"

"Draw aside the curtain and you will see a grater."

"There is no picture here."

"But there is a grater." He kept a snuff-grater behind the curtain on purpose.

His dependence on snuff became notorious. David Edwin, the engraver, tells us that once when he was waiting in Stuart's drawing-room, his host entered in great agitation, passed Edwin without a greeting, and began to rummage in a closet. The visitor, who had experienced the painter's terrible temper, thought he must have offended him; he watched uneasily while Stuart found some tobacco, a grater, and a sieve. Although his hands trembled so violently that he could hardly hold his instruments, Stuart managed to grind some powder. After he had inhaled it noisily, his un-

common tremor abated. Then he turned to Edwin
with a smile. "What a wonderful effect," he said, "a
pinch of snuff has on a man's spirits!"

When the Roxbury house was sold over Stuart's
head, the new owner, Mrs. Robert Hooper, had the
greatest difficulty getting him to leave. He was finally
driven, in 1817 or 1818, to Washington Place on
Fort Hill, an eminence which then overlooked the
harbor but has since been leveled. In 1823 he rented
from a tailor a three-story brick structure at 59 Essex
Street.

He would certainly have been more prosperous
had he traveled more widely, gone again to New
York, Philadelphia, and Washington, where a new
generation of faces awaited his pencil; visited the other
cities of the expanding United States. Massachusetts
had harbored the eccentric genius so long that he had
become boring. His incompetence in money matters,
with its occasional overtones of chicanery; his bursts
of temper; and that fact that the most abject begging
could hardly secure a portrait in less than three years
were irritations which Bostonians found it increasingly
difficult to bear. His style no longer communicated the
excitements of novelty, and people who found themselves less impressed than when they had first seen his
work whispered that his eye had lost its accuracy, that
he had grown too old to paint.

Stuart had, it is true, grown careless. When it was

brought home to him that he was less admired than he had been, he would paint a portrait or two with special attention. In 1816 he told Jouett: "I have often, very often roughened my second or third sitting that I might be thrown back and, having to use more color, produce a richer effect. The reason why my paintings were of a richer character thirty years ago: then it was a matter of experiment. Now everything comes so handy that I put down everything so much in place that for want of opportunities . . . [I] lose the richness."

Quality, however, was not the basic issue; many Bostonians would rather be painted by someone new, even if the result were inferior. Chester Harding, a physical giant from the Ohio Valley who had come to Massachusetts to seek advice from Stuart, was amazed when his own painting-room became "a place of fashionable resort, and I painted the enormous number of eighty heads in six months." Harding had to turn away an equal number of applications, while "Mr. Stuart was allowed to waste half his time in idleness for lack of sitters. I can account for this public freak," the lucky artist wrote, "only in the circumstance of my being a backwoodsman newly caught. Then the circumstance of my being self-taught was trumpeted about much to my advantage." As an older man, Harding considered that the portraits he had sold in such quantities were no more than "tolerable," and even in 1822, the year of their rivalry, he considered himself vastly inferior to Stuart. But he could only apologize to the master and Stuart could only ask non-paying visitors to his empty studio: "How goes the Harding fever?"

It was inertia, not love of Boston, that kept Stuart from striking out for virgin markets. Lonely, out of place in the self-styled "Christian Sparta" that was preparing for a moral renaissance, he loved to recall gay evenings he had spent in London, in Philadelphia, where every good fellow had emptied four or five bottles as a matter of course. He irritated self-consciously cultured Bostonians by referring to Philadelphia as "the Athens of America." How sardonically he laughed when he could not persuade them that he was not joking!

Since his son's death, Stuart's family had been entirely made up of women. In 1816 his daughter Emma, who is said to have been a painter, was married to a Mr. Stebbins, but that left Mrs. Stuart; Agnes, who was fast turning into an old maid; the adolescent Ann; and Jane, a little child. In this dove-cot Stuart set up a perpetually male disturbance; he called his wife "Tom" and Jane "Boy." Knapp noted that he dominated the household so completely that it had an aggressively masculine air.

According to Neagle, Stuart seemed basically unhappy, but he loved to converse, "had a fund of anecdote, and was then cheerful." Although he made his pupil feel completely at his ease, "his family," so Neagle noted, "appeared to fear him."

His youngest daughter, Jane, wrote: "Stuart had by nature an irritable temperament, which many circumstances were calculated to make still more irritable. The constant interruption to which he was subjected became exasperating. . . . While he was engaged with his whole soul in portraying the character of some remarkable person, the door would be besieged by persons who must see him, and frequently for the most trifling purpose. At times he would be so disturbed as not to feel like going to his painting-room again for the whole day." (Sully put the matter differently: "He was a very capricious man, and would never paint unless he was in the humor, although the way is to begin, and the humor will come afterwards.")

Her father, Jane continued, found that when he received all callers, he could not get his work done even if he stayed in his studio, without refreshment, "from ten o'clock in the morning until seven o'clock in the evening. . . . Finally, he would receive only some favored friend, after having been occupied in painting all morning. This, of course, made him enemies."

Jane dwelt on Stuart's most admirable quality, that gentleness to the humble which was the other side of his anger with the proud: "Anything like adverse fortune or neglected merit was sure to find a place in his regard. It was a standing rule of the house, if such or such persons came to call, they were not to leave without receiving some hospitality. A musician, a poor dusty trumpeter, whose merits had never been acknowledged by the public, . . . used to call on Stuart. He would give him a good dinner, and then talk upon musical subjects for hours afterwards. . . . A comfortable addition would be made to his pocketbook."

Concerning another pensioner, an old Revolutionary soldier, Agnes Stuart once asked her mother: "Why does my father always pay Major J—— for dining here?"

Jane insisted that her father would not paint on Sunday unless pressed, but she could recall only one occasion on which when he accompanied his ladies to church. He remained standing during the sermon, leaning nonchalantly against the side of the pew and inhaling huge pinches of snuff. " 'Well,' he said on the way home, 'I do not think I shall go to church again. . . . I do not like the idea of a man getting up in a box and having all the conversation to himself.' . . .

"Nothing delighted him more than teasing my mother whenever he could find an opportunity for doing so. She was a remarkably intelligent and cultivated woman, though a matter-of-fact person, and this sort of quizzing was carried too far. Stuart took the greatest pleasure in teasing her by telling her the most extraordinary stories with such a serious countenance that it was impossible to know if it was really the case or not."

Once, after talking with the farmer who supplied the family with poultry and eggs, Stuart entered the parlor with a grave face. "Green," he said tragically, "is going to die."

"Going to die?" cried Mrs. Stuart. "He is well enough. Why do you say so?"

Stuart shook his head. "Green is going to die."

"Why, Mr. Stuart, what do you mean? Green is as well as you or I."

"Green, nevertheless, is going to die. I know it, for he has just returned to me ten dollars I overpaid him."

When Jane tried her own hand at such spoofing, Mrs. Stuart expressed anger. "I have been annoyed enough with your father's nonsense in this way. Besides, it is very bad taste."

That Mrs. Stuart was dissatisfied is indicated by her reluctance, reported by her daughter Ann after Stuart's death, "to talk of things gone by." She herself may not have been easy to get on with. Henry Fay, a friend of Stuart's who tried to help her in her widowhood, was stopped by her objections to every expedient he suggested. "One is so much disgusted with such folly," he burst out, "as to abandon such people to their fate." He complained bitterly of Mrs. Stuart's "ingratitude."

Life with father did not encourage the Stuart girls to get married, and Emma, the only one who took the risk, saw it end unhappily. Nine years after her wedding she was living in Boston as "Mrs. Stebbins," but she is next heard of as "Miss Emma Stuart," an invalid under medical care in Providence. The records of Trinity Church, Newport, give the date of her death as November 19, 1875, her age as eighty-five, and contain no hint that she ever had a husband.

The mother and the other three daughters ended their days in one household at Newport. Surviving the painter by seventeen years, Mrs. Stuart died in 1845, aged seventy-seven. Agnes followed her five years later. Ann and Jane lived on together for so long that they became a local legend.

Ann spent her time "seated on a sofa listening, occasionally uttering a quiet reproof to Jane." Tall, quiet, and frail, she seemed, years before her death in 1868, to be "fading out of life by slow degrees." A local young lady, Mary E. Powel, tells how once Ann claimed that her dim eyes saw "something like a veil full of sparks of fire falling over my prosaic face and figure. . . . 'Be quiet, Ann,' urged Miss Jane, but I thought that a child of Gilbert Stuart might see more than others."

Jane was a reincarnation of her father, although hampered by being a woman and possessed of little talent. She had the "bold lionlike features" that made everyone take him at sight as a man of note; they merely made her ugly. Once a masher, seeing from behind her girlish figure, her firm stride, and her beautiful feet, hurried after her at night. Under a street lamp, she turned her face to him—and smiled sardonically, as her father might have done, to see his confusion. Telling the story with no audible sigh, she commented: "An angel to chase; a devil to face."

A favorite of Newport society, Jane faced down the millionairesses in their diamond tiaras wearing a tiara she had self-manufactured from black velvet and artificial pearls. At a charade, she did not object to being type-cast as a gorilla, the missing link in a bearskin robe; but before the evening was out she reappeared in a court dress, the strong, erect body under her ugly face graceful in a minuet.

With other women, Mary E. Powel remembers, "she had many intimacies, sometimes overstrained. Occasionally there were sudden ruptures. Faults probably on both sides." Her mainstay was "her old handmaiden Isabella," buxom, eccentric, gypsy-like. The daughter Stuart had called "Boy" died in 1888.

For sixty years she had supported herself and the other Stuart women by creating portraits and copying her father's *Washingtons*. That her skill in no way rivaled his she realized, and sometimes she complained bitterly that he had kept her too busy grinding colors to give her any instruction. Stuart had learned nothing from his son's tragedy. When Neagle asked him why he failed to encourage Jane's ambitions, he replied that you throw a presumptive Newfoundland puppy into the river: if of the true breed, he will swim without being taught.

As a girl, Jane happened in the family attic on the portrait of Mrs. Jerome Bonaparte Stuart had abandoned when he had quarreled with Napoleon's brother: "the stretcher had been taken from it, and the canvas, unrolled, was lying on the floor." Thinking it very beautiful, Jane started a surreptitious copy; her heart stood still when she heard her father's footsteps on the stair. He appeared in the garret breathless, stared at her for a moment, shouted that the chimney was on fire, and disappeared through a trap door to the roof. In terror at what he had caught her doing, Jane sat with the guilty copy before her, awaiting his rage when he returned. But Stuart demonstrated again the unpredictability of his nature: "Why, Boy, you must not mix your colors with turpentine. You must have oil."

Jane had little opportunity to learn even the most rudimentary things. To enter her father's painting room in his absence was forbidden, and his attitude toward interruptions made it, as she wrote, "a settled thing in the house that it was best to abstain altogether" unless specifically invited. At first she had thought that when her father was safely out of the house, she could tiptoe in and look around without danger. But Stuart had set up too efficient a machine. "The arrangement of his painting-room was simple," Jane said years later, "more simple than any other painting-room with which I have been familiar." Since everything was placed exactly where he wished it, he knew on his return if anything had been touched, and responded with horrifying anger. The most heinous sin of all was to pick up one of the brushes on which he lavished the most devoted care.

Although he could still summon his courtly manners when he wanted them, Stuart no longer had the patience to dress neatly. John Quincy Adams considered him "highly picturesque, with his dress always disordered, and taking snuff from a large round tin wafer box, holding perhaps half a pound, which he must use up in one day. He considers himself beyond question the first portrait-painter of his age, and tells numbers of anecdotes concerning himself to prove it, with the utmost simplicity and unconsciousness of ridicule. His conclusion is not very wide of the truth."

The first portrait-painter of the age: this was the distinction he had always sought, but now that the years were closing to him doors that could never be opened, he wondered whether it was enough. He knew that historical painting, the "grand style" of figure art which had been practiced by his master West, was still regarded as the only true road to the peak of Parnassus; he often spoke to Knapp of his "strong desire to do something in the historical way to leave behind me." This proved to be no more than an insubstantial yearning, but in his sixty-sixth year he did paint his only known landscape and a genre-like composition of a boy chasing butterflies. The pictures were not successful, and he never deviated from heads again.

Stuart remained one of the narrowest specialists among highly talented artists. In his specialty, his skill deteriorated surprisingly little, although Neagle tells us that "his hand shook at times so violently that I wondered how he could place his brush where his mind directed." Another eyewitness described how "Stuart stood with his wrist upon the rest, his hand vibrating, and when it became tolerably steady, with a sudden dash of the brush he put the color on the canvas."

During his seventy-first year, Stuart completed a portrait of John Adams, and charmed the ninety-year-old ex-President into softening his prejudice against painters. "Speaking generally," Adams said, "no penance is like having one's picture done. You must sit in a constrained and unnatural position, which is a trial to the temper. But I should like to sit for Stuart

from the first of January to the last of December, for
he lets me do just what I please, and keeps me constantly amused by his conversation." When Stuart
showed the finished portrait to one of his friends, he
said: "Look at him. It is very like him, is it not? Do
you know what he is going to do? He is just going to
sneeze."

Later that same year, Stuart suffered a stroke that
paralyzed his left arm and the left side of his face.
Gout joined with paralysis to make his life an unceas-
ing round of pain.

Now the specter of leaving his wife and daughters
destitute, which had long haunted him in depressed
moments, became his constant companion. No one
could blame him for not having been prolific—he had
in his lifetime produced some thousand portraits—
and he had received good prices—a minimum of
$100 for a bust, $150 if he went to the waist. The
trouble was, he decided, that "a man who works with
his hands can never become rich. A grocer will make
more by buying a cargo of molasses in a day than my
labor can bring me in a year."

When he hobbled around the house, it was clear
how little he had to leave behind. The furnishings of
his painting-room—easel, stool, table, looking-glass,
old carpet, six cheap chairs, shovel, tongs, and fender
—were excellent for their purpose, but would hardly
bring much money. In the parlor were his best things:

an organ (later assessed at $100), books ($45), a case of instruments ($15), a good carpet, looking-glass, and fire set. But the twelve chairs were shabby ($33\frac{1}{3}$ cents apiece), as were the teaboard and waiter. All that was worth much in the back parlor was the clock ($7), although the table with ends ($5) was not too bad. In the kitchen, the kitchen chamber, the back chamber, and the four chambers on the second floor the furnishings did hardly more than serve necessity. He had little silver beyond the teaspoons ($7.70) and his snuffbox ($3.50).

In answer to a request that he undertake another full-length of Washington, he got someone to write— his own hand was too shaky for anything but wavering down a signature—that he would do so if his health improved. He would want two years to complete it, $2,000, and the exclusive right for fourteen years to have an engraving made. He worked on smaller pictures, slowly and painfully, yet with amazing effect.

When in 1828 he became too sick to rise, the doctors said his gout had settled on his chest and stomach. For three months he suffered mounting agony. Calling one day, Washington Allston was horrified to see how emaciated was the body that lay rigid on the bed. Solicitously he asked Stuart how he was. A ghost of the old scornful smile appeared on the unparalyzed side of Stuart's face. "Ah," he cried, "you can judge." He drew his pantaloons up to show his shrunken leg. "You can see how much I am out of drawing." A few weeks later, on July 9, 1828, he was dead.

Stuart left assets of $375, debts of $1,778. Although Philadelphia's leading artists agreed to wear mourning for a month in his honor, although the newspapers gave much space to his praises and expressions of national loss, his funeral was a quick, cheap, family affair. In a cut-rate coffin, his remains were stowed in a vacant space in the Central Burying Ground, bought from some tradesmen who had a bigger vault than they needed. His family instantly forgot where he had been buried. A friend, Jane explained, wrote down the number of the vault during the interment, but lost the piece of paper. The information was available in the municipal death records, but his wife and daughters announced firmly to inquirers that his bones had been permanently mislaid. No monument, not even the simplest stone, marked Stuart's last resting-place.

Thus sadly a great painter passed from the national scene, and with him passed the great days of American portrait art. Between the first years of settlement and the death of Stuart, our painters, although they had tried their hands at other things, had been primarily creators of likenesses. Portraiture went on, of course, and produced its specialists, but the major interest of

the most interesting painters turned from man to nature. In a green tidal wave of foliage, the romantic
movement broke over American studios.

Stuart had lived through wild years. Molten lava
seethed in correct-seeming breasts covered with linen
ruffles, until at last forces long constrained erupted
into two revolutions. While the artist watched, a
civilization that had been sickening died, and a new
stood up in its cradle and screamed with the fury of
an infant.

On the surface, Stuart was a Georgian gentleman,
habitué of drawing-rooms, yet he was swayed by the
maladies and inspirations of romantic artists. In con-
duct, he was as close to Turner as to Reynolds. His
life reflected the conflicts of the generation into which
he was born, and so did his work. Opening his eyes
when the eighteenth century had but half unrolled,
he believed the proper study of man was man. Living
through the first quarter of the next era, he saw men
not as types, but as individuals, each worthy of study
because of a personality uniquely his own. A product
of transition, he imprisoned under glass the butterfly
of change. On panel and on canvas he recorded brilliantly the faces and characters of the voyagers who
shot one of the great rapids in the river of history.

BIBLIOGRAPHY

THIS book is a completely revised and greatly expanded version of the biography of Gilbert Stuart in James Thomas Flexner's *America's Old Masters* (New York, 1939).

No important collection of Stuart papers has ever been found; he was too careless to preserve any documents, too impatient to write any long, revealing letters. What little material his family may have preserved was destroyed when Jane Stuart's studio burned down during the nineteenth century. A few Stuart letters may, however, be seen at the Pennsylvania, the Massachusetts, and the New-York Historical Societies. Harry MacNeill Bland, who has assisted me in many ways, owns photostats of Stuart documents that have passed through his hands. Hall Park McCullough, also of New York, possesses various Stuart papers, including the book of notes kept by Matthew Harris Jouett when he was studying in Stuart's studio, the most important single source concerning the painter's ideas on art.

The mill where Stuart was born still stands near Jamestown, Rhode Island. It has been restored, and fitted up with snuff-grinding machinery of the period.

William Dunlap's *History of the Rise and Progress of the Arts of Design in the United States* (2 vols., New York, 1834; new edition edited by Frank W. Bayley and Charles E. Goodspeed, 3 vols., Boston, 1918) contains, in addition to Dunlap's own recollections of Stuart, accounts of him by a number of his associates, including the essay by Dr. Waterhouse which is the most reliable source of information concerning Stuart's youth. Although the picture of Stuart drawn in this book is not flattering, it tallies well with independent contemporary accounts and may be taken at face value. That Dunlap himself suppressed some of the more damaging anecdotes he received may be seen by consulting his *Diary, 1766–1823*, edited by Dorothy C. Barck (3 vols., New York, 1931).

Jane Stuart published three articles about her father in *Scribner's Monthly* (XII, 1876, pp. 367–74; XIII, 1876–7, pp. 640–6; XIV, 1877, pp. 376–82) which give the family's version of his career, and her own memories of his character.

Stuart's daughter Ann contributed a short sketch of her father to Wilkin Updike's *History of the Episcopal Church in Narragansett* (3 vols., Boston, 1907). This work also quotes from church records important source material concerning Stuart's childhood.

William T. Whitley's *Gilbert Stuart* (Cambridge, Mass., 1932) contains a large amount of new material, primarily about Stuart's English and Irish periods. Mr. Whitley's investigations in contemporary newspapers are particularly important.

The most up-to-date information about Stuart's paintings is to be found in the files of the Frick Art Reference Library. I am grateful to this institution and also to the New-York Historical Society for much assistance.

Lawrence Park's *Gilbert Stuart, an Illustrated Descriptive List of His Works* (4 vols., New York, 1926) is a monumental work of scholarship, although, as every work of this magnitude must, it contains errors. Two of the large volumes are made up of catalogue, two of reproductions. An excellent short biographical sketch of Stuart by John Hill Morgan and an appreciation by Royal Cortissoz are included.

In "Some Unrecorded Portraits by Gilbert Stuart" (*Art in America*, XXI, 1932–3, pp. 15–27, 39–48, 81–96) William Sawitzky makes many new attributions to Stuart and corrects errors in Park's catalogue. He states that about a hundred pictures listed there, or roughly ten per cent, are misattributions. See also William Sawitzky's "Lost Portraits Add to Gilbert Stuart's Fame" (*New York Times Magazine*, August 12, 1928).

George C. Mason's *The Life and Works of Gilbert Stuart* (New York, 1879) comprises a rudimentary catalogue of the painter's work and a lengthy biographical sketch which contains some previously unpublished material obtained from Stuart's daughters, but pays for this privilege by glossing over the unpleasant details of his life and character.

The most important source concerning Stuart's Irish years is J. D. Herbert's *Irish Varieties of the Last Fifty Years* (London, 1836). When Herbert and Dunlap report Stuart's speech, they give it exactly the same flavor; the artist's way of talking must have been very marked to have made so deep an impression.

For a short account of Stuart by one of his Boston friends who had a deep psychological insight into the painter's tortured character, see Samuel L. Knapp's *American Biography*, volume 3 of his *The Treasury of Knowledge and Library of Reference* (New York, 1855).

An eloquent account of the history behind Stuart's painting of Augusta Montagu may be found in Booth Tarkington's *Some Old Portraits* (New York, 1929).

Stuart's portraits of Washington are catalogued and discussed by John Hill Morgan and Mantle Fielding in their *Life Portraits of Washington and Their Replicas* (Philadelphia, 1939). An earlier volume of similar intention, Elizabeth Bryant Johnston's *Original Portraits of Washington* (Boston, 1882), is, of course, less up-to-date, but contains some material not elsewhere published. See also Charles Henry Hart's *Catalogue of the Engraved Portraits of Washington* (New York, 1904) and Charles Allen Munn's *Three Types of Washington Portraits* (New York, 1908).

John Hill Morgan's *Gilbert Stuart and His Pupils* (New York, 1939) gives biographies of many of the young men who worked in Stuart's studio, and contains a complete transcript of the notes Jouett kept concerning Stuart's teaching.

Much information on Stuart's later years is contained in two articles by Mabel M. Swan: "Gilbert Stuart in Boston" (*Antiques*, XXIX, 1936, pp. 65–7) and

"Paging Gilbert Stuart in Boston" (*Antiques*, XXXIV, 1938, pp. 308–9).

Wilbur D. Peat, director of the John Herron Art Institute, Indianapolis, kindly supplied me with the information I have used about Stuart's pupil Lewis Peckham.

INDEX

A NOTE ON THE TYPE

This book was set on the Linotype in a face called *El-dorado,* so named by its designer, WILLIAM ADDISON DWIGGINS, as an echo of Spanish adventures in the Western World. The series of experiments that cul-minated in this type-face began in 1942; the designer was trying a page more "brunette" than the usual book type. "One wanted a face that should be sturdy, and yet not too mechanical. . . . Another desideratum was that the face should be narrowish, compact, and close fitted, for reasons of economy of materials." The specimen that started Dwiggins on his way was a type design used by the Spanish printer A. de Sancha at Madrid about 1774. Eldorado, however, is in no direct way a copy of that letter, though it does reflect the Madrid specimen in the anatomy of its arches, curves, and junctions. Of special interest in the lower-case letters are the stresses of color in the blunt, sturdy serifs, subtly counterbalanced by the emphatic weight of some of the terminal curves and finials. The roman capitals are relatively open, and winged with liberal serifs and an occasional festive touch.

This book was composed, printed, and bound by The Plimpton Press, Norwood, Massachusetts. Paper manu-factured by S. D. Warren Company, Boston. The typog-raphy and binding were designed by the creator of its type-face—W. A. Dwiggins.